FIVE ESSAYS FOR
FREEDOM

A political primer for animal advocates

Kristy Alger

REVOLUTIONARIES
Brisbane, Australia

This book has been non-blind peer reviewed by an
industry professional

ISBN 978-0-6450486-0-5 (Paperback)
ISBN 978-0-6450486-5-0 (eBook)

Cover image by Jo-Anne McArthur
Book design by Paula Pomer
Typesetting by Oda Tolsrød

First published in 2020

Revolutionaries
Brisbane, Australia
www.revolutionaries.com.au

FIVE ESSAYS FOR
FREEDOM

A political primer for animal advocates

Other titles from Revolutionaries

Acknowledgements

This book was written on the lands of the Mumirimina people, on country east of the Kutalayna. I wish to acknowledge their Elders, past, present and emerging. I honour their strength and their survival in the face of an ongoing occupation, and the strength and survival of the many Aboriginal nations across this vast and ancient continent. I honour the oldest living culture on this Earth. This always was and always will be Aboriginal land.

To my husband, you are my heart.

To my children, you are my soul.

To my parents, for raising me to be political and argumentative.

To my sister, for arguing with me.

To Wallea and Dyann, for giving this work wings.

To my friends and supporters, for every word and every act of love.

To the animals, who are friends, family, survivors, and freedom fighters.

In a time of great trials, tribulations and trauma, to find joy in you all is an act of resistance.

And to the untold numbers of slaughtered beings whose voices remain as yet unacknowledged.

I hear you.

Contents

The politics of life

"Laws are like cobwebs, which may catch small
flies, but let wasps and hornets break through."
— *Jonathan Swift (1801/2015)*

In 1986 I lived for some months in Bundaberg, in an old house raised on stilts situated next to a vast sugar cane field. My memories of this time are few and fleeting, being both very young and somewhat forgetful. I remember the car-flattened corpses of cane toads desiccated in the sun, which enthralled me and terrified my older sister. I remember the sounds and smells of sugar canes crackling in the summer heat. And I vividly recall the warnings of my parents, to not run through the cane fields; snakes, spiders and unknown dangers lurked there and were to be avoided.

It was an invitation to adventure for two wayward 80s kids.

There was an abandoned house on the edges of the cane fields, a colonial ruin that was like a magnet to my sister and I. It reeked of risks and stories, making us feel like we were in our very own Nancy Drew novel. Ignoring the bindies catching in our socks (which were the tell-tale signs of wrongdoing picked up by our mother) we would race towards that house, anticipating what we might find inside. Smugglers, rumrunners, maybe even a murder? But we were always disappointed.

The only danger we encountered, anchored within the empty double frame of the front doorway, was a massive spider web.

We never saw the spider or spiders who created this web, but we were always on edge imagining just how big they had to be, or how many of them might be hiding in the dusty corners waiting to ensnare us. This was an unfounded arachnophobia which has unfortunately stayed with me into adulthood. But while there was fear, there was also respect. This web was not only massive, it was also intricate and strong. Each thread connected to another in a network of lines upon which the entire web complex depended for communication, structure and survival. And ever present, the creators themselves who were hidden from view but never far. Always ready to repair or extend the web where necessary, or to consume those who became entangled within its threads.

The memory of that web has always stuck with me, no matter how forgetful I have remained into adulthood.

Decades have passed and the house and the web no longer exist. Undoubtedly the sugar cane fields eventually subsumed them both as the demands of industry expanded across the landscape. But in my later life I have begun to see other types of webs that are no less intricate but are more predatory. These are the webs of political complexes that define and control every aspect of our lived experiences in an increasingly industrialised world. I was raised in a political household by parents who insisted that my sister and I watch the news every night or read anything other than the latest teen novels. They achieved this with varying degrees of success. However it was not until I chose to become vegan that other animals began to feature in my understanding of politics. It has taken me some years to progress beyond the somewhat naive apoliticism that defined my earliest forays into veganism towards a politically informed commitment to anti-speciesism. To be apolitical is defined as being politically neutral, and without having a political attitude, content or bias (Collins Dictionary, 1999).

Veganism is an ethical standpoint that rejects the ideologies that are used to justify the exploitation of other animals for human profits, pleasure, tastes and traditions. In particular, it challenges the ideology of speciesism which is based on prejudice against other animals who are viewed as having less intrinsic value compared to humans (Ross, 2020). Veganism advocates for the adoption of nonviolent consumer behaviours or ideological standpoints that do not necessitate or allow for the exploitation of other animals.

This encompasses not using animals for food, entertainment, research and clothing and includes changing social attitudes towards a nonviolent and respectful relationship between humans and other animals (Francione & Charlton, 2013).

Veganism involves a commitment to work towards the goals of nonviolence and non-use of other animals by individuals and socio-economic institutions (Eaglehawk, 2020) in practicable ways. It is important to note here the difference between the word *practical* and *practicable*, with the former relating to the actual doing of something, and the latter relating to that which is able to be done successfully.

This is a crucial distinction to make, as it makes allowances for those areas of human life where an impact upon other animals cannot be avoided whilst establishing the framework necessary for animal advocates in their struggle for change. As a result targeting the individual whose circumstances may necessitate a continued use of animals is avoided. For example, this ethical leeway may be afforded to individuals who require particular medications. It can also be afforded to people who live in nutritional deserts where access to adequate nutrition is restricted by financial inequality, regional locations and government policies that result in the marginalisation of individuals and communities. Within this practicable framework it is important to advocate for change in these circumstances by campaigning for the social, medical and technological advances necessary to cease animal exploitation where it is as yet unavoidable. Further, practicable veganism brings the focus to the social,

economic and political systems that perpetuate the exploitation of other animals. In turn, this avoids blaming disempow-
ered individuals and communities for systems they were not
responsible for creating. Thus, veganism becomes an ethical
standpoint against the politics of animal exploitation without
further entrenching the marginalisation of disadvantaged
individuals and communities. In many ways veganism can
be used as a tool to contribute to human liberation alongside
animal liberation with potential benefits for social justice,
public health and environmental sustainability.

I did not understand this when I first went vegan and
became involved in animal rights activism nearly a decade
ago. It was not until I became involved with the diverse and
radical individuals at Animal Liberation Tasmania that the
true nature of the socio-political landscapes I was operating
within became apparent to me. I came to realise every aspect
of the human existence is political, including the myriad ways
society as a whole impacts upon other animals and the natural world. Now I find myself in seemingly constant conflict
with government authorities and with the many industry
groups whose profit margins are extracted from the lives and
bodies of other animals. I have spent years of my life butt-
ing heads with bureaucrats and business owners. Alongside
this, I've been engaging with other people of a more radical political disposition, and seeking out the diverse voices
discussing the politics of life itself. My former understanding
of veganism was a reductionist apolitical conceptualisation
that focused on convincing others to go vegan like me. It

was without any consideration for the nuances of politics that shape humans' everyday existence. I wholeheartedly embraced veganism as an *identity* rather than as an ethical standpoint or as a tool to utilise in the fight to deconstruct oppressive systems. I bought the t-shirts, followed the mainstream vegan leaders and spent hours of my time fighting with non-vegans on the internet without any understanding of the history or political importance of veganism.

Politics is not simply a question of which major party an individual votes for. I see this as a limited understanding of politics and how it affects our daily lives. Rather, I think there is a need to discuss politics as comprising the vast networks between the state, institutions and corporations of society. These networks extend throughout human communities and beyond like a vast spider's web occupying every doorway an individual might seek to walk through. Access to food and water, clothing, education, transport, housing, healthcare, jobs and opportunity are determined by the situation of birth. For example, in some areas of the United States of America (US) and Canada, neighbourhoods with a higher proportion of Black, migrant or Indigenous residents may be subjected to systemic discrimination. This occurs through what is known as 'redlining' where various government and private sector services fail to make financial services, healthcare, even access to supermarkets accessible to disadvantaged social groups (Caves, 2005). Further, the quality of life and the expressions of interpersonal relationships are determined by the politics of legality with legislators creating laws that define the validity of those relationships. For example, the marriage equality debate in Australia in 2017 resulted in the legalising of same-sex marriage but only after concerted nationwide campaigning by individuals and activist groups (McKeown, 2018). Concerningly, how citizens participate in democratic processes such as protest and dissent, and the resulting consequences, can be altered with the stroke of a legislator's pen. In 2019 the Tasmanian Liberals reintroduced anti-protest laws that criminalise acts of protest which target businesses and also grant police alarming powers, such as waiving the requirement to issue a move on order before making arrests (Tasmanian Government, 2019). For the overseas reader I would like to note that in Australia 'liberal' means left-of-center, whereas the Liberal Party (state and federal) are a right-of-center conservative party. The Liberal Party are neoliberal in their ideology and policy, however so too are their opposition, The Labor Party.

Since the 1980s neoliberalism has become entrenched in the Australian political system to the extent that all major parties will formulate policies within the neoliberal paradigm. This has included support of the animal agriculture industry even by the Greens, who are positioned as the left-of-centre environmentally conscious alternative to the Labor/Liberal divide. Neoliberalism is the political ideology of free-market capitalism associated with the privatisation of public institutions, the deregulation of industries and the globalisation of markets via free-trade agreements (Harvey, 2005). It is also associated with cost-saving austerity measures that undermine social welfare and result in the commercialisation of poverty and inequality (Harvey, 2005). Neoliberal government policy is designed to create the market environments necessary for industry and corporations to flourish and promotes the manifestly fallacious notion of trickle-down economics (Stockhammer, Constantine & Reissl, 2015). This dominant idea of economics refers to the creation of wealth by corporations and an elite few which will result in the 'trickling down' of some wealth for the majority of the population. However, the Australian Council of Social Services (ACOSS) reports that the wealth of the top 20% of Australians has increased by 68% in the past 15 years, whereas for the bottom 20% it has increased by a mere 6% (ACOSS, 2020). This is evidence that trickle-down economics has failed and will continue to fail. Thriving communities require equitable access to services, resources and wealth, not the sequestering of that wealth by the corporate elite (Baum, 2015).

There can be no such thing as apoliticism in a world constructed and defined by politics. This is especially apparent when considering the social movements dedicated to the pursuit of justice and rights for humans, other animals and the Earth, such as the animal rights movement. Unfortunately, discourse in the animal rights movement has become centred on promoting an apolitical vegan message that denies the role of interconnected networks of politics in perpetuating the ongoing exploitation of, and violence towards, other animals. The populist ideology of vegan consumerism, largely promoted by charismatic 'celebri-vegans' (often to their own financial advantage), has become the mainstream focus of the movement. This is evidenced to the extent that corporations actively involved in the exploitation of other animals are praised and promoted so long as they create products for vegans to consume. As more people become drawn to the strategically filtered image of veganism successfully promoted by social media influencers, the reality of the animal exploitation landscape is obscured.

Politics is about power, and can typically relate to the government or the public affairs of a country. However, the concept of politics also relates to those actions taken in the interests of status and power of dominant social groups, organisations or political parties (Mills, 1956). Thus, at the heart of government support (federal, state and local) for animal agriculture, land ownership and animal research and breeding facilities, lies the pursuit of power. This unequal power dynamic is reinforced by the lobbying of increasingly powerful industry representative groups, such as Meat & Livestock Australia (MLA). For example, the manufacturing of the Australian identity as a nation 'riding on the sheep's back' refers to the reliance of the Australian economy upon the wool trade since colonisation began (Cashin & McDermott, 2002). As a result, farmers have long been idolised as the backbone of the nation. Though Earle Page may have been the caretaker Prime Minister for a short 19 days in 1939, as leader of the Country Party (from 1921 to 1939) he was the primary architect of the working coalition between his party and the Nationalist Party. The former became the National Party of Australia, and the latter became the Liberal Party of Australia. As Mayes states:

> Earle Page […] used the notion of "country-minded-ness" to argue that Australia depended on farmers and graziers for its high standard of living. It was also the farmers who forged the core elements of the national character by taming the environment, making it productive, and creating a home. (2019, n.p.)

The farmers' ability to tame and cultivate the land renders them economically invaluable for a settler-coloniser nation. Inter-relatedly, they have become an important national symbol that politicians frequently seek to emulate as a means to appear authentically 'Australian.' For example, politicians are often in the media wearing the iconic Akubra hat (that is today made from the mostly imported skins of industrially farmed rabbits), or posing with farming equipment in rural settings (Mayes, 2019).

Thus, the pursuit of animal liberation necessitates more than a simple changing of individual hearts and minds and the increased availability of plant-based options. Advocates for other animals need to also actively work towards the dismantling of an inherently colonial mythology. This mythology has become so pervasive that even those who do not claim fervent allegiance to the nation will stridently defend their perceived right to consume other animals as a part of the Australian identity. The MLA have successfully manipulated that mythology through their Australia Day marketing campaigns aligning the celebration of a nation with the increased consumption of lamb flesh. The campaigns appeal to depictions of diversity in the community in a superficial representation of the socio-political makeup of those communities, including the appropriation of Indigenous culture and identity and the white-washing of colonial history.

The 2017 MLA Australia Day campaign depicted Aboriginal people hosting a barbeque on the beach and welcoming colonisers to the shore, who brought gifts of food and beer, eventually culminating in a large 'inclusive' party centred around the cooking of lamb flesh (MLA, 2017a). These advertisements were, in part, paid for by contributions made through taxpayer dollars distributed to the MLA by the Australian government (MLA, 2017b). The public's money is at work manufacturing a cultural identity that is reliant upon the violence that has been historically inflicted and continues to be inflicted upon others within a coloniser system that encourages consumption over compassion or critical thought. Further, for many Aboriginal peoples the celebration of the so-called Australia Day public holiday marks the beginning of ongoing colonisation, genocide and dispossession and is deeply offensive (Haughton, 2018). Annual Invasion Day protests (held on the same date) draw increasing numbers of supporters every year.

In this primer I aim to provide an understanding of these networks and systems, the web of politics that entrap individuals irrespective of their engagement with it. Even the spider who creates the web is so wholly dependent upon it that they cannot be extricated. My goal is to provide an investigation into systems and structures, to analyse statistics and to combine history, philosophy, even some psychology and personal musings. I will construct a critique of animal advocates' tactics and strategies as a means forward and to dismantle these exploitative structures. The investigation takes the form of essays that do not follow the more commonly understood format of modern academic writing. Rather they resemble the idea of the essay first conceptualised by the French philosopher Michel de Montaigne (1533-1592) who combined personal anecdote, his role as a statesman and intellectual insights to create his major work *Essais* (Montaigne, 1580). The word 'essay' itself is derived from the French infinitive *essayer* meaning 'to try.' This is my goal, to try to contextualise the socio-economic and political systems and contexts, utilising both formal and informal writing techniques. The primer will give the reader what I hope are valuable insights into the political landscape as a means to become better strategists, to improve established forms of advocacy and activism, and to create new ideas. Because if there is one area the mainstream vegan movement fails it is in a lack of the active promotion of a culture of questioning and criticism, without which progress cannot occur. Sometimes in order to build something stronger, citizens must tear down that which is already falling.

An understanding of the politics of animal exploitation is critical for the realisation of animal liberation. Advocates for other animals operate in an environment where increasing attacks on education under neoliberal policies, such as the 2020 hikes on Australian university fees targeting the liberal arts proposed by the Liberal National Party (Karp, 2020), have combined with the promulgation of quick-consume online sources of information and all too often, disinformation. For example, the Journalism and the Pandemic Survey of 2020 identified Facebook as the most prolific source of online disinformation (Posetti, Bell & Brown, 2020). As such, it is critical that accessibility is created to the resources necessary for the animal advocate's understanding of the politics of animal exploitation. This is essential to strategically disrupt the webs of corporate government that guarantee the continuation of animal exploitation, to the detriment of other animals, humans and the Earth.

The first essay will lay the foundations of questioning, critique and understanding upon which animal advocates can build for the future. I will commence by examining the concept of the animal industrial complex which was initially defined by Noske in her work *Beyond boundaries* (1997). This involves describing the totality of relationships between the state, industry, institutions and society that further entrench the continued exploitation of other animals. I will work through examples of how the animal industrial complex manifests primarily in Australian politics and society, but with some references to the US and the impacts on countries in South America as a means to contextualise my argument.

In the second essay I will address how the scope of veganism and the animal rights movement can, and indeed must, include issues often dismissed as irrelevant to the struggle. Veganism needs to include human rights and environmental causes within its scope due to their intersectionality with animal rights (Ross, 2020). In order to be most effective in creating change throughout the broader community it is useful to understand the differences between focusing on one issue and a scope that embraces all the complexity of related ethical issues. Thus, veganism is not diluted by the inclusion of issues not directly relating to other animals but is rather strengthened by it. The third essay includes a consideration of the human construct of the justice system as the carceral state which stands in opposition to the fundamental ideals of animal liberation. In essay four, I will propose ideas for ways to break out of the web of vegan consumerism. This web within a broader complexity of webs has been created through reliance upon social media as well as individual and group activist politics, which I will argue encourages the isolation of the activist from the broader community. In the fifth essay, I will deconstruct the notion of the activist identity itself and the issues inherent within the adoption of this identity. Finally, I will conclude that the way forward is to acknowledge the agency of other animals and to facilitate their role as the leaders of their own resistance.

Throughout this work I will refer to animals as 'other animals' as a means to delineate between human animals and other animals. At the same time, the term reduces that distinction by emphasising how animals are other animals along with humans. Some advocates choose to refer to them as 'non-human' animals, while others may choose not to attempt to distinguish between humans and other animals at all. All of these approaches are fraught with issues. Non-human may establish human as the dominant norm. And other as a descriptor may be perceived to effectively exclude other animals from society by 'othering' them. As yet I do not feel we have developed a language that is capable of succinctly expressing the complexities of how we should refer to other animals, but the definition is important as it delineates between the oppressor group (humans) and the oppressed (other animals). Thus I choose to refer to animals as other; they are other to humans as they have been othered by humans, and they are other animals along with humans. But there is work to be done to create a language of animality that makes the social space accessible to other animals.

This book is named for animal advocates. The animal advocate community is wide and diverse; not all vegans advocate for the rights of animals and not all animal advocates are vegan. I was personally involved with the rescue of other animals before I embraced veganism. Advocacy can include a specific focus on individual animals or groups of animals, such as wildlife rescue, or specific industries such as the live export trade. At many of the rallies I have attended against the live export trade key speakers (mostly politicians) have not been vegan, and have actively promoted a message in support of the domestic trade in animal farming. And many vegans support a version of animal rights that is inherently welfarist, that is to say focusing on incremental changes to the treatment of other animals rather than advancing the abolition of animal exploitation in its entirety. For the non-vegan animal advocate, this book will provide the ethical and political reasons why veganism is important. For the already vegan, or those on their way towards veganism, I aim to provide the tools for understanding the politics of animal exploitation and for creating effective strategies moving forwards. And for the reader who is neither vegan nor an advocate for other animals, I hope this book provides the reasons for why you should become both.

I am of the opinion that accessibility is the key to creating a just world; accessibility of information, of community, and of opportunity. To that end, the animal rights movement must extend its scope beyond the promotion of apolitical vegan consumerism which given the connections between government and corporations cannot be factually described as apolitical. A practicable veganism ethical framework which encompasses animal rights, human rights and environmental sustainability is a multi-strategy means to create that accessibility for the realisation of justice. As citizens who are animal advocates we can begin pulling at the intersecting threads of the animal industrial complex, progressing towards a future where we ourselves are freed from the web alongside the other animals we seek to advocate for.

Finally I ask you all to read with care. Many of the concepts and situations discussed in this book contain descriptions of violence towards other animals. These may prove distressing to the reader, as empathetic individuals who may already be struggling with the burden of the systems of violence we are striving against. But I will work to also offer you hope, and show how these systems can be dismantled one thread after the other.

References

Australian Council of Social Services (ACOSS). (2020). *Poverty in Australia 2020: Part 1 overview.* https://newsroom.unsw.edu.au/news/social-affairs/unsw-and-acoss-report-shows-3m-Australians-living-poverty

Baum, F. (2015). *The new public health.* Oxford University Press.

Cashin, P., & McDermott, C. J. (2002). 'Riding on the sheep's back': Examining Australia's dependence on wool exports. *Economic Record, 78*(242), 249-63. DOI: 10.1111/1475-4975-4932.00055

Caves, R. W. (2005). *Encyclopedia of the city* (1ˢᵗ ed.). Routledge.

Collins Concise Dictionary (4th ed.). (1999). Harper Collins Publishers.

Eaglehawk, W. (2020). Species justice is for every body. In D. Ross, M. Brueckner, M. Palmer & W. Eaglehawk (Eds.), *Eco-activism and social work: New directions in leadership and group work* (pp. 100-110). Routledge.

Francione, G., & Charlton, A. (2013). *Animal rights: The abolitionist approach.* Exempla Press.

Harvey, D. (2005). *A brief history of neoliberalism.* Oxford University Press.

Haughton, J. (2018). *A short history of Australia Day and Aboriginal and Torres Strait Islander reactions to it.* https://www.aph.gov.au/About_Parliament/Parliamentary_Departments/Parliamentary_

Library/FlagPost/2018/January/Australia_Day_Indigenous_ reactions

Karp, P. (2020). *Australian university fees to double for some arts courses, but fall for stem subjects.* https://www.theguardian. com/australia-news/2020/jun/19/australian-university-fees- arts-stem-science-maths-nursing-teaching-humanities

Mayes, C. (2019). *Cultivating a nation: Why the mythos of the Australian farmer is problematic.* https://theconversation.com/ cultivating-a-nation-why-the-mythos-of-the-australian- farmer-is-problematic-106517

McKeown, D. (2018). *Chronology of same-sex marriage bills intro- duced into the federal Parliament.* https://www.aph.gov.au/ About_Parliament/Parliamentary_Departments/Parliamentary_ Library/pubs/rp/rp1718/Quick_Guides/SSMarriageBills

Meat & Livestock Australia (MLA) (2017a). *New MLA lamb campaign launches with a celebration of Australia.* https://www. mla.com.au/news-and-events/industry-news-archived/2017/ new-mla-campaign-launches-with-a-celebration-of-australia/#

Meat & Livestock Australia (MLA) (2017b). *Annual report 2017- 18.* https://www.mla.com.au/about-mla/how-we-are-governed/ Planning-reporting/annual-reporting/annual-report-2017-182/#

Mills, C. (1956). *The power elite.* Oxford University Press.

Montaigne, M. (1580/1992). *Essais de messier Michel de Montaigne.* M. A. Screech (Trans.). Viking Adult Press.

Noske, B. (1997). *Beyond boundaries: Humans and animals* (revised ed.). Black Rose Books.

Posetti, J., Bell, E., & Brown, P. (2020). *Journalism & the pandemic: A global snapshot of impact.* https://www.icfj.org/our-work/journalism-and-pandemic-survey

Ross, D. (2020). Speciesism. In S. Idowu, R. Schmidpeter, N. Capaldi, L. Zu, M. Del Baldo, & R. Abreu (Eds.), *Encyclopedia of sustainable management.* Springer. https://doi.org/10.1007/978-3-030-02006-4

Stockhammer, E., Constantine, C., & Reissl, S. (2015). Neoliberalism, trade imbalances, and economic policy in the Eurozone crisis. *Nova Economia, 25*(special edition), 749-75. https://dx.doi.org/10.1590/0103-6351/3551

Swift, J. (1801/2015). A tritical essay upon the faculties of the mind. D. Swift, T. Sheridan, & J. Nichols (Eds.), *The works of the Rev. Jonathan Swift, Volume 5.* Palala Press.

Tasmanian Government (2019). *Workplaces (Protection from Protestors) Amendment Act 2019.* https://www.justice.tas.gov.au/community-consultation/closed-community-consultations2/workplaces-protection-from-protesters-amendment-bill2019

Unravelling the animal industrial complex

At first, the socio-political and economic webs humans are ensnared in may seem too large and too established to be successfully deconstructed. As the individual wealth (and associated power) of a handful of elites increases exponentially even during a global public health crisis (Woods, 2020) it seems impossible to unravel the threads. The task becomes ever more onerous as the dollar signs multiply. However, webs can be broken. In this essay, I will begin to uncover how the web is connected and interconnected, comprising an expansive animal industrial complex that has its roots in the industrial revolution. By providing analytical examples of how this complex manifests within the Australian corporate and political context I will provide insights to assist animal advocates in recognising how the complex operates. I will also use examples from the US as a means to provide a global context to how the animal industrial complex manifests in Australia.

Industry and government have long maintained a relationship of power and private profit. In the 18th century, English landlords began adopting the more efficient farming techniques that had been practiced in Holland and Northern Belgium since the early 17th century. However, for these practices to be effectively established it was necessary for parliament to intervene and pass enclosure acts in order to consolidate the many smaller commons into larger tracts of arable land (Wolloch, 1982). Between 1760 and 1851, 3600 such acts were passed by parliament comprising six million acres of land (Wolloch, 1982). As a result of improved technologies and the passing of these enclosure acts, diversification of the types of other animals used for flesh, fibre and labour and more efficient techniques for the fattening of those animals for market became possible (Wolloch, 1982). This enabled the establishment of larger herds, with a greater access to fertilisers and a constant cycle of productivity on the land.

The social and physical structures of rural communities which prior to the state enforcement of enclosure acts had utilised the commons for subsistence cropping altered dramatically. This resulted in the mass exodus of the population from villages to urban centres (Breunig, 1977). Here the people dispossessed of their lands would seek employment within the burgeoning manufacturing centres. The combination of greater labour populations with advances in technologies such as the Spinning Jenny and water wheels altered the cottage-based textile manufacturing systems, replacing them with the high production factory (Breunig, 1977). Commensurate to this growth was the increase in the administrative personnel required to oversee governance at all levels of manufacture and trade (Breunig, 1977). From its infancy, industry has been reliant upon the interventions of government for opportunity and advancement. The industrial revolution created the foundations of contemporary socio-economic and political systems.

However, it was not until after World War II, with the US advances in corporate and military interests, that the concept of the industrial complex became defined. As Best states:

> By the mid-twentieth century, in sectors ranging from medicine, agriculture, media and entertainment, to security, education, criminal justice and transportation, virtually all institutions were reconceived and reconstructed according to capitalist, industrial, and bureaucratic models suited to the aim of realizing profit, growth, efficiency, mass production and standardized operations. (2011, p. xvi)

Industrial complexes are socio-economic systems in which industry, government and institutions become inextricably connected in order to create the economic environments necessary for a profits-driven economy. The concept describes the totality of the connections, relationships and operations undertaken by industry and government in pursuit of market creation or expansion. This expansion has often occurred to the detriment of human, other animal and non-animal communities. Each defined complex is connected to the next, forming a vast and intricate web of industry, economy, and society, wherein every facet of the industrialised experience is reliant upon another. Nibert provides the following example of this relationship:

> The animal industrial complex also is intertwined with the medical industrial complex, as the treatment of conditions and diseases stemming from the socially manufactured 'meat'-based diet results in billions of dollars in profits. (2011, p. 207)

In turn, the animal industrial complex overlaps with the medical industrial complex which refers to the political and industrial networks between pharmaceutical companies, the educational sector and government. It also overlaps with the academic industrial complex which encompasses the relationships between government, tertiary institutions and the corporate bodies who utilise them for research. Government investment in universities is utilised to fund experimentation on other animals for research into conditions that afflict humans. Industry lobby groups pay for research into animal agricultural markets, science and industry innovation utilising government institutions such as the Commonwealth Scientific and Industrial Research Organisation (CSIRO).

Since the 1980s, contemporary neoliberal ideology has dominated Australian government interactions with industry to the extent that the role of government is limited to providing the requisite resources for industrial advancement.

As Harvey writes:

> The state has to guarantee, for example, the quality and integrity of money. It must also set up the military, defence, police and legal structures and functions required to secure private property rights and to guarantee, by force if necessary, the proper functioning of markets. Furthermore, if markets don't exist (in areas such as land, water, education, health care, social security, or environmental pollution) then they must be created, by state action if necessary. But beyond these tasks the state should not venture. (2005, p. 2)

The effects of neoliberal ideology can be seen in Australia through the effective privatisation of welfare through the creation of a cashless debit card system that arguably enables private company Indue Pty. Ltd. the ability to profit from people's poverty (Wilson, 2020). Under this system the majority of individual welfare payments are no longer deposited directly into the recipient's personal bank account and are instead quarantined to a government allocated debit card. Money on the card cannot be withdrawn via an automatic teller machine, nor can it be spent on tobacco, alcohol or gambling. The card is limited to use at a number of major corporate retail giants thus depriving the welfare recipient of being able to purchase second hand goods via cash or online (such as school uniforms or furniture), or to pay for school camps or excursions that require cash only payments. This effectively denies welfare recipients an equality of access to affordable products and services, thus entrenching poverty further rather than assisting people towards financial autonomy and responsibility (McIlroy, 2020).

The program also forms an integral part of the ongoing economic colonisation of Australia, as the card was initially trialled in communities with a higher Aboriginal population (Heaney, 2019). The majority of people whose payments have been quarantined under the scheme are Aboriginal or Torres Strait Islander people (Young, 2020). Former National Party president Larry Anthony was a director of Indue between 2005 and 2013 (Hardy, 2019). Similarly, ARL Collect (Pty. Ltd.) was awarded a contract worth $3.3 million (all dollar figures are in AUD unless otherwise stated) by the Department of Human Services to collect debts generated by the Liberal National Party's controversial and socially destructive Robodebt scheme (Bajkowski, 2019). Under this scheme tens of thousands of welfare recipients received large debts based on an inaccurate automated analysis of their incomes. Many recipients no longer had the paperwork necessary to prove the inaccuracy of the debt or were unable to repay the debt itself.

Poverty is big business; so too is pollution. Carbon trading schemes, which have been touted as the panacea to the climate crisis, have instead resulted in the effective commodification of atmospheric pollution by industry. As Shiva states:

> Polluting the atmosphere is an enclosure of the
> commons. What was once a resource available to all
> has been privatised by the oil and coal companies,

the automobile and power companies, as a place to
dump their pollutants [...]. Through emissions trading, private polluters are getting more rights and more
control over the atmosphere, which rightfully belongs
to all life on the planet. (2011, pp. 184-85)

Corporations are now able to conceal their carbon out-
puts through systems of trade and credits with few tangible
decreases in output but with very real increases in profits.
Meanwhile, the federal government continues its attacks on
the tertiary education sector through funding cuts and redis-
tributions that force universities to move towards business
models, with clients rather than students, and a focus on creating a labour resource for industry rather than as centres of
higher learning and often radical political agitation (Barcan,
1998). Where markets did not previously exist, neoliberal
politics have created them. Countries such as Australia have
moved beyond the capitalist model of 'everything must have
a function' towards the neoliberal model of 'everything must
have a price.'

In the late 80s Dutch cultural anthropologist Noske
defined the animal industrial complex in *Beyond boundaries: Humans and animals* as a socio-economic and political system that combines government with agribusiness,
research and development in pursuit of corporate interests
and the creation of markets. She writes that:

Farming systems are not developed as an answer
to public demand but predominantly as a result of

expensive research, aimed at cost reduction, carried
out by agricultural scientists and financed by big business or governments. (Noske, 1997, p. 23)

Production does not meet demand, rather government
and industry collude to create markets and saturate those
markets with supply, using myriad institutions as a means
to encourage increased productivity and consumption.
Between 1933-39, under President Franklin D. Roosevelt's
New Deal economic programs, US producers of soy and corn
were paid by the government to reduce their surplus product
(Nibert, 2011). Producers instead used these payments to
increase productivity and thus the surplus, the solution to
which became the use of the surplus corn and soy as a means
to increase meat production and the application of taxpayer
funds to encourage increased consumption of animal flesh
(Nibert, 2011). The concentrated animal feeding operation
(CAFO) was born, with government and industry turning to
the emerging broadcast media to artificially create consumer
choice and guarantee a market for high volume products
(Nibert, 2011). This is a relationship that continues to this day,
not only through the saturation of advertising for fast and
junk food products on TV, but also through the presentation
of advertising as news.

In 2018 I researched the backgrounds of four health
experts who appeared on the Seven Network's morning
program Sunrise and the Nine Network's Today Show, who
were invited to provide critiques of plant-based milks. All
four individuals were vocal supporters of increasing dairy

consumption for health and all four were actively involved with the Dieticians Association of Australia, whose corporate partners at the time included Meat & Livestock Australia (MLA) and Dairy Australia. The contents of these segments were promoted as being factual and without bias irrespective of the connections with industry lobby groups. This can be viewed as evidence of how these lobby groups are able to utilise the media to encourage (or discourage) consumption behaviours to promote usage of their products.

Despite the foundations of modern industrialised animal exploitation in the collusion between industry and government, the concept of the animal industrial complex has primarily received attention from scholars and authors engaged in the sphere of Critical Animal Studies. The concept has rarely enjoyed extensive attention within the mainstream vegan movement as the average YouTube video. This needs to change as animal advocates' understanding of these structures is essential to being able to dismantle them. It is more than just being able to recognise the names and faces operating on behalf of industry or within government. Rather, this understanding opens individuals' eyes to the webs in front of them and enables them to begin pulling at all these interconnected threads. There are a number of reasons why collapsing these webs has become a necessity, not least at all for the benefit of other animals. Deconstructing the animal industrial complex can facilitate the collapse of many of the industrialised iterations of animal exploitation, such as farming or vivisection (experimentation conducted on living animals). However, there are other benefits that would result, such as environmental or health benefits, which would affect society through an extensive re-imagining of the social space.

When the English parliament first began implementing enclosure acts in the 18th century, they effectively established a system that enabled the sequestering of public lands and resources to the financial and political benefit of a small number of people. This was to the detriment of the local communities who depended upon access to that land, often for their very survival. Enclosure acts continue to this day, under a number of guises and impact upon both human and other animal communities. For example, fish feedlots (farming facilities used for the intensive rearing of animals) have been established in public waterways throughout Tasmania, with leases granted to private companies such as Huon Aquaculture and Tassal by the government. In 2020 the Tasmanian Alliance for Marine Protection released information revealing these companies are not paying true market value for these leases, costing the state $2 billion per annum in lost revenue that they say could be used to better oversee the industry (Powell, 2020). The public are now restricted from accessing these areas, including local Aboriginal groups who are the traditional custodians of the land. There are also increasing reports of environmental issues impacting human and other animal communities.

The primary function of the animal industrial complex is to establish the market, political and social environments necessary to guarantee a small handful of individuals can create maximum profits and power bases for themselves. This comes at the expense of the broader community, including other animal communities. The animal industrial complex, and the other industrial complexes with which it intertwines, guarantee that resources, lands and money are transferred, via a network of legislation, taxation and subsidisation, from public access into private hands. The entrenchment of industrial complexes, as a key focus of neoliberal governments, seeks to convince broader society of the validity of trickle-down economics. That is to say, if private corporations are given maximum access to profit-making opportunities, money will make its way into the pockets of the poor. However, the divide between rich and poor continues to increase. The 2017-18 survey on income and wealth by the Australian Bureau of Statistics (ABS) showed an increase in income inequality that in 2018 created an economic drag with a social cost to the nation of up to $8 billion (ABS, 2018). Deconstructing these industrial complexes thread by thread, including the animal industrial complex, is not only a necessity for the actualisation of other animal liberation. It is also a necessity for the establishment of a fair and equitable society that allocates resources according to actual need rather than to those who want to increase their profit margins in pursuit of stakeholder satisfaction.

Twine augmented the original definition of the animal industrial complex to describe it as a:

> [...] partly opaque and multiple set of networks and relationships between the corporate (agricultural)

sector, governments and public and private science.
With economic, cultural and social and affective
dimensions it encompasses an extensive range
of practices, technologies, images, identities and
markets. (2012, p. 23)

The public passing by can see the large sheds of the chicken
farms, the lambs in the fields, and the signs outside of the
slaughterhouses. However, the visibility of operations that
turn sentient beings into products is obscured and rendered
opaque by the fences, gates and enforced distances between
the public and the facilities. They are also obscured by the
various social and economic politics that govern and support
the expansion of animal exploitation industries, including
the introduction of laws that increase penalties for investigators and activists alike. The animal industrial complex is not
exclusive to the relationship of government and industry in
the manufacturing of food (flesh, milk, eggs) or textiles (wool,
skins, silk). It includes the industries and markets that are
involved in the exploitation of other animals for: entertainment (circuses, racing, zoos, aquariums, television and film);
animal companion ownership (breeding and sale of pets,
including exotics); the hunting of non-domesticated animals
(including the permits and contracts for culling); the 'pest'
extermination industry; the breeding of and trade in other
animals for experimentation including vivisection, and; the
breeding of other animals in service including but not exclusive to for use by the carceral system. The animal industrial
complex is so pervasive in human society that most people

do not see it. Exploitation of other animals has become a normalised facet of the human experience (Eaglehawk, 2020) to the extent that even the adoption of vegan ideals cannot fully extricate the individual from its influence.

Rather than focusing on an analysis of the work of others, I will instead here attempt to demonstrate how the animal industrial complex manifests in Australia through a series of examples of government interventions and industrial relationships, and the interactions between both that create market access for industry. The examples I will provide are by no means the only observable manifestations of the animal industrial complex but are rather examples and analyses in two key areas, industry funding and the public record, to refer to as foundational knowledge that will assist in the animal advocate's own investigations. I encourage the reader to take what is offered here merely as a means to begin recognising other manifestations around the animal industrial complex, and to commence the work necessary to dismantle those apparent systems where possible.

Federal government and animal agriculture sector funding

The Australian system of animal agricultural sector funding differs from many global counterparts in that producers are amongst the least directly subsidised in the world. According to a report released by the Australian Bureau of Agriculture and Resource Economics and Sciences, subsidies as a direct percentage of farm revenue in Australia currently sit at 2% (Greenville, 2020). Greenville writes:

> Government support is now dominated by invest-
> ments in sector capacity, such as R&D [research and
> development]. Where direct support is provided, it
> is concentrated on risk management tools to help
> manage Australia's uniquely variable climate. These
> tools include Farm Management Deposits and
> income tax smoothing. (2020, p. 4)

A significant proportion of industry sector funding is
delivered indirectly via a system of matched government
research and development funding schemes. This system
sees millions of dollars granted to what are effectively industry lobby groups (including the MLA and Dairy Australia)
who engage in research, innovation, marketing and policy
creation. This is referred to as general services funding and
constitutes approximately half of the $3 billion agriculture
funding policy of 2018-19 (Greenville, 2020). Under statu-
tory agreements, levies are collected from individual producers and paid to the government. These levies are then paid
to the lobby groups, which are organisations established to
promote the interests of the industries they represent, along
with a matched government contribution. The category of
agriculture must be understood to encompass both animal
and plant production systems. However, the grain, corn and
soy industries cannot operate independent of animal industries, and vice versa. The animals used to feed the human
population must themselves be fed also.

The following figures are drawn from the 2018-19 annual
reports of just some of the primary animal agricultural

industry representative organisations that are in receipt of these contributions (the figures do not include additional grants or emergency funding):

- Meat & Livestock Australia (MLA, 2019): $80 900 000
- Fisheries Research and Development Corporation (FRDC, 2019): $23 000 000
- Dairy Australia (DA, 2019): $20 058 000
- AgriFutures (AF, 2019): $17 777 000
- Australian Pork Ltd (AP, 2019): $5 018 132
- Australian Meat Processors Corporation (AMP, 2019): $4 285 561
- Australian Eggs Ltd (AE, 2019): $3 513 966.

In the 2018-19 financial period, the MLA utilised these matched government contributions to invest over $170 million in research and development projects in partnership with government corporate entities including the CSIRO and the tertiary education sector (MLA, 2019). Dairy Australia spent $58 million on industry innovation, research and marketing, including five separate programs targeting children and young people through school programs, namely, Dairy Path, Cows Create Careers, Young Dairy Network, Discover Dairy Online for Primary Schools, and Picasso Cows for Schools (Dairy Australia, 2019). These programs guarantee access to a seemingly inexhaustible supply of new consumers and create new potential labour markets for the industry, effectively institutionalising the exploitation of other animals via the publicly funded education sector. Perhaps the most pernicious of these programs is the Picasso Cows scheme, where schools are gifted a fibre cast model of a cow for students to decorate in return for access to the school curriculum through the provision of educational materials that provide a humane-washed perception of the dairy industry whilst encouraging students to consume more dairy for health. This is despite the increasing evidence that indicates that dairy intake may be associated with adverse health risks, including a 2020 report that associates dairy intake with an increased risk of breast cancer (Fraser, Knutsen, Sirirat, Maschak, Orlich, & Jaceldo-Siegl, 2020).

Sector funding also exists to expand the operations of individual privately owned businesses. In 2019 Tasmanian Quality Meats (TQM), the subject of a 2017 exposé by the Farm Transparency Project, Animal Liberation NSW and Animal Liberation Tasmania, was granted $8 million by the federal government (Morris, 2019). The grant was secured by former Nationals Senator Steve Martin as part of a $50 million boost for the Tasmanian meat processing sector (Morris, 2019). It enabled the slaughterhouse to increase kill rates from 350 000 sheep and lambs per year to 750 000 head annually with no mention of the dairy calves who are also slaughtered at the facility (Morris, 2019). This would reduce overheads for local producers who were already in receipt of $5 million per year in subsidies under the Tasmanian Freight Equalisation Scheme (TFES) export scheme, a government funded subsidisation scheme providing equal opportunity for industries to compete in other markets (TFES, 2020). TQM had already been in receipt of three grants under the

2012 Tasmanian Government Innovation and Investment Fund totalling over $1 million (Workabout Australia, 2012). In 2018, the company struck a deal with the Tasmanian Liberals to take over operations at the Devonport City Abattoir along with $400 000 of government funding (the remainder of an $800 000 grant to the previous operator, the Brazilian owned corporate giant JBS (Wilkins, 2018; Hosier & Coulter, 2018). And in October 2020 it was announced that the Tasmanian Liberal's would be granting $2 million towards the construction of a $3 million pig killing factory in Scottsdale, to be owned and operated by Scottsdale Pork (Ferguson & Barnett, 2020). In questions posed to the state premier Peter Gutwein, the Green's leader Cassy O'Connor raised concerns over the granting of funds to a company owned by a member of the Exclusive Brethren (a deeply conservative subset of the Chrsitian evangelical movement), which she claimed pay no taxes (O'Connor, 2020).

Other privately owned facilities across Australia have been and continue to be the recipients of government grants. In 2014 Luv-a-Duck received $600 000 to expand operations at their facility in the Victorian town of Nhill (Twomey, 2014). In 2020 Northern Co-operative Meat Co. received $1.5 million in federal government funding for the development of retail ready products (McCormack, 2020). Schmidt Grazing Industries received a grant of $250 000 from the Palaszczuk Labor government to construct a 20 000 head sheep feedlot in Queensland's Southern Downs (Sheep Central, 2020). The federal and the Tasmanian state governments contributed

$247 000 and $250 000 respectively to pay for the Northern Midlands Business Association truck-wash at Powranna in 2018 (Rockliffe, 2016). The primary objective was to prevent the spread of disease between cattle and sheep many of whom are held at the nearby Powranna and Cressy cattle and sheep feedlots, or sold at the adjacent Robert's Livestock Marketing Complex (Baker-Dowdell, 2017). These are merely a handful of the examples of grants and funding provided directly to privately owned companies by state and federal governments as a means to expand operations and increase productivity. The cumulative result is an increase in the numbers of other animals exploited and slaughtered for the meat industry alone. Government financial contributions are made across the animal exploitation sectors, including live export markets.

In 2019 the deaths of hundreds of dairy cows exported to Sri Lanka by Wellard Live Export Company were revealed by the Australian Broadcasting Commission (Knowles & Heanue, 2019). Wellard have been involved in some of the most high profile live export scandals reported in recent years, including cruelty to other animals (Wahlquist, 2019). The company's former general manager was convicted for the falsification of commonwealth documents which allowed a consignment of 22,000 sheep to be imported into Pakistan in 2012 where they were brutalised and some were reported to have been buried alive (Perpitch & Weber, 2018). The dairy cows exported by the company in 2019 were part of a dairy industry establishment program whereby the

Australian government via the government operated Export Finance and Insurance Corporation (EFIC) underwrote a series of loans to the Sri Lankan government worth $100 million for the purchase of dairy cows by local producers in the region (Knowles & Heanue, 2019). Wellard had been contracted to transport 20 000 cows between 2012 and 2019; by April 2019 only 5000 had been shipped (Knowles & Heanue, 2019). Despite being checked by industry vets, 500 of the cows died either en route or once in Sri Lanka due to malnutrition and disease including Bovine Viral Diarrhoea (Knowles & Heanue, 2019). Those who survived did not produce the promised amount of milk, in some cases less than half of the projected output (Hettiarachchi & Deane, 2019). Farmers reported losing entire herds, having to cull both adults and calves, and facing bankruptcy; there were reports of farmers becoming suicidal (Knowles & Heanue, 2019). The Sri Lankan auditor-general joined farmers and animal rights advocates in calling for an end to the scheme saying it was poorly planned and inhumane (Knowles & Heanue, 2019). These calls were rejected and Wellard blamed the deaths on what they described as a small number of farmers who refused to accept the training they were supposed to supply (Knowles & Heanue, 2019). In May of 2020 the former Sri Lankan opposition leader Sajith Premadasa urged the government to suspend the program (News First, 2020). Instead the Sri Lankan government approved the importation of another 2500 heifers under the scheme (News First, 2020).

In a statement to the ABC, EFIC claimed it had no involvement with the scheme beyond the facilitation of the $100 million in loans:

> EFIC provided the facility after the transaction was deemed to meet the necessary International Finance Corporation's Environmental, Health and Safety Guidelines. The cattle were also inspected and certified by Australian authorities and accepted by veterinarians from the Sri Lankan government before departure. (Knowles & Heanue, 2019, n.p)

The role of government in this scheme was to provide finance and the rubber stamp; any intervention beyond this would not be accepted. In April 2019 the Australian government initiated a ban on the live export of sheep to the Middle East during the northern hemisphere summer following the release of footage of maltreatment and suffering from the El Awassi live export ship (Fisher, 2019). The ban was condemned by producers, exporters and pro-live export politicians alike, resulting in a lifting of the ban later that year (Fisher, 2019). In seeking to act on issues of animal welfare in live export, the Australian government had arguably overstepped the boundaries of their role. Their willingness to refuse considering a permanent ban or even enacting a permanent partial ban due to industry pressure is worrying evidence of the power corporations hold over government.

The Sri Lanka dairy scheme can be viewed as an act of economic colonisation, the effective invasion of another country via industry and trade deals. Under the animal industrial complex, intervention in foreign markets and production is a tactic that has been utilised by imperialist nations for many years. Between 1970 and 1987, the World Bank (based in Washington DC) granted loans worth $463USD million to establish or expand cattle ranching projects throughout Bolivia, Ecuador, Uruguay, Paraguay, Colombia, Chile and Brazil with the purpose of making these regions key suppliers of beef to Europe and the US (Nibert, 2011). Nibert states:

> Moreover, in 1971 the UN Food and Agricultural Organization recommended that Latin American nations begin cultivating food grains for export, and the U.S. tied food aid to food-grain export production. US corporations such as Cargill and Railston Purina received low interest government loans to facilitate food-grain production in Latin America. (2011, pp. 203-4)

The results were devastating because the scheme effectively resulted in enclosure acts that forced subsistence farmers from their land and relocated entire rural and Indigenous populations into urban areas. Transnational corporations exploited them as a cheap labour resource resulting in social and cultural deprivation and profound poverty (Nibert, 2011). This is reminiscent of the massive social shifts caused by the implementation of enclosure acts in the 18th century. US imperialist policies have created the enclosure of commons throughout South America where Nibert (2011) states many subsistence farmers who refused to leave their lands were murdered. The violence has continued in the years since. In 2013 an Argentinian woman, Sofia Gatica, was targeted by gunmen in her own home in reprisal for her campaign against the indiscriminate use of glyphosate by Monsanto in neighbouring soy fields (Graves, 2012).

In 2018, 97.9% of all soy meal imported into Australia was grown in Argentina (Observatory of Economic Complexity (OECD), 2018). The vast majority of this was used in feed for farmed animals including fish, cattle, sheep and chickens (OECD, 2018). The Australian animal agricultural system is potentially complicit in the ongoing social and environmental injustices caused by the production of soy in that region. By channelling public funds directly into lobby groups whose programs are designed to maximise the consumption of other animals, the Australian government is effectively making the broader community complicit. The complicity is not only in the abuses and exploitation of animals on our own shores but in potential human and other animal rights abuses overseas and the environmental degradation of vital ecosystems. Even those of us who have chosen to live vegan are implicated through our unavoidable engagement with the taxation system. In this way our taxes effectively cancel out our veganism, rigging the system against any changes veganism may potentially have when it is defined as a purely consumer-based ideology.

The same economic and political principles that formed the foundations of the US and European push into South America are apparent within the scheme to increase dairy production in Sri Lanka. The scale may be smaller but the impacts are no less profound as is intended by the very system itself. Shiva states:

> Industrial agriculture, sold as the Green Revolution and 2nd Green Revolution to Third World countries, is a chemical-intensive, capital-intensive, fossil fuel-intensive system. It must, by its very structure, push farmers into debt, and indebted farmers everywhere are pushed off the land, as their farms are foreclosed and appropriated. In the poor countries, farmers trapped in debt for purchasing costly chemicals and non-renewable seeds sell the food they grow to pay back debt. That is why hunger today is a rural phenomenon. The debt-creating negative economy of high cost industrial farming is a hunger-producing system, not a hunger-reducing system. (2011, p. 173)

What was sold to Sri Lankan farmers as a viable alternative to expensive powdered milk was arguably a hunger-producing system, not a solution. Farmers are now bankrupt, their lands at risk of forfeiture due massive debts to the Sri Lankan government who in turn is in debt to the Australian government credit agency (Knowles & Heanue, 2019). This situation provides a foothold in the region for further market interventions to the benefit of corporations and industries active in Australia, including Wellard. The only option for many farmers in Sri Lanka other than land forfeiture may be to take on further debt under the scheme, in the hope that next time the end results will be different.

Protest, laws and the public record

Australian state and federal parliamentary debate is recorded in the Hansard which is a series of important historical documents that constitute a public record of the dialogue that takes place within the houses of parliament. Members' words are recorded verbatim, sometimes edited to remove repetitions or to correct mistakes without detracting from the meaning of what was said (Australian Parliament House, 2020). The Hansard has recorded parliamentary debate in Australia since federation on January 1st 1901, when the separate states and territories came together under one federal government. The ability to access and scrutinise the information documented in the Hansard is an important facet of the Australian democratic process as it contains valuable insights into the working relationships between government and industry bodies. As well as, of particular relevance here, recording prevalent attitudes towards activists and activism groups for posterity.

In 2019 the Tasmanian Liberal state government proposed amendments to the Dog Control Act in response to a series of attacks on little penguins, and the bill was opened to the public for comment. The following debates relating to the amendments are documented in the Hansard. Local organisation Animal Liberation Tasmania (ALT) had contributed a submission that was largely in support of the amendments, which placed greater responsibility on the custodians of dogs found to be at large in protected areas. On the 10th of October 2019, Labor member of parliament Anita Dow quoted two brief sections from the ALT submission during parliamentary debate, in relation to increasing the numbers of rangers monitoring little penguin colonies and the inclusion of cats under the proposed legislation. The following day the Minister for Primary Industries Guy Barnett used the parliamentary debate to launch a lengthy and scathing attack on Dow and ALT, labelling the organisation disruptive extremists who had caused significant damage to the reputation of animal agriculture in Tasmania. Barnett demanded that the Labor party stand to condemn ALT on the public record, in defence of regional and rural industries (Appendix 1a). Earlier that day, Barnett had stated during debate over the Tasmanian Liberal's long-term plan for Tasmanian agriculture that "we are working shoulder to shoulder with the Tasmanian Farmers and Graziers Association [TFGA] and the Tasmanian Agricultural Productivity Group [TAPG]" (Appendix 3a).

The TAPG is an industry organisation that connects primary producers, food and non-food agricultural manufacturers, forestry and agribusiness with the government. The aim is one of ensuring continued and increased productivity, multi-sector approaches to issues affecting Tasmanian agriculture and to reinforce public confidence in the safety and quality of Tasmanian produce with an emphasis on animal production systems (TAPG, 2020). The TFGA is the peak body representing the interests of Tasmanian farmers and graziers at a state and national level, maintaining affiliations with Australian Dairy Farmers, Cattle Council of Australia, Sheepmeat Council of Australia, Wool Producers Australia and Meat & Livestock Australia. Their goal is to create policy and funding for research and development as well as to lobby for direct financial support for industry from the government (TFGA, 2020). This relationship between a key government department and what is effectively an industry lobby group extends into the animal welfare sector. When the Royal Society for the Prevention of Cruelty to Animals (RSPCA) Tasmania required a new CEO they appointed former TFGA CEO, whose appointment was publicly welcomed by the Minister for the Department of Primary Industry (DPI) (Barnett, 2020). RSPCA Tasmania is financially dependent upon a DPI contract totalling $550 000 per annum, and the organisation had previously ceded responsibility for animal welfare cases involving animal agriculture to the DPI under a Memorandum of Understanding with the department. This relationship arguably undermines the independence of an organisation whose role is to intervene and investigate neglect and cruelty to other animals.

The statements made by Barnett regarding ALT and his verbal attacks on Dow that are recorded in Hansard cannot be divorced from his prior comments on those close working relationships he and his department have with industry lobby groups such as the TAPG and the TFGA. His words appear as a deliberate ploy to undermine the integrity of ALT and those who seek to dissent against government and corporate control. Further, it is arguably a strategic attempt to undermine the validity of the organisation's concerns by using the public record in a manner that would be somewhat suited to the McCarthy era in the US which had its origins in the 40 and 50s. During this time a political attitude developed that was centred on opposition to elements held to be subversive (primarily communism) by those in authority and the application of tactics involving personal attacks on individuals, communities and organisations by means of widely publicised indiscriminate allegations especially on the basis of unsubstantiated claims (Storrs, 2015).

Just as public scrutiny of the Hansard is an important facet of the Australian democratic process, so too is public access to a free and impartial media. However, government and corporate influence and control has eroded the integrity of the Australian media to the extent that it now often represents little more than a platform for government and industry propaganda to manipulate public discourse to their own advantage. Mass advertising during prime time television by corporations such as McDonalds, KFC and Dominos pushes consumerism and animal exploitation into homes uninvited. In August 2020 multiple media outlets published a story purporting to be news that claimed dairy milk was better for the environment than soya milk (Morrison, 2020). After a brief investigation it transpired the article was little more than advertising for a farming lobby group called Sustainable Food Trust, an organisation largely made up of farmers and agribusiness members whose primary goal is research and development, and policy advocacy for industry (Sustainable Food Trust, 2020). This was not the first article of its kind and has since proved to be far from the last, as vitriolic reporting on vegans and animal rights activists seems to be a selling point for a media that profits from controversy. But the violence of anti-vegan and anti-protest rhetoric promoted by the Australian media was never more apparent than in April 2019, following the Dominion Documentary day of action. This nationwide protest event involved government office occupations, street protests, slaughterhouse lockdowns and the now infamous shutdown of the Melbourne city centre by protestors locked to immobilised vans (Murphy, 2019).

Almost immediately, politicians began using the media to malign the activists involved, in an attempt to undermine the validity of their cause and appeal to the manufactured populist ideals of individual choice and unlimited consumerism. Prime minister Scott Morrison was variously quoted as calling the activists involved shameful, green-collared criminals, as being un-Australian and he claimed that the protest action itself ran "against the national interest, and the national interest is farmers being able to farm their own land" (McCulloch, 2019, n.p). These statements hark back to the coloniser farming mythology as a means to perpetuate the connection of national identity with eating meat that has been so successfully utilised in advertising by the prime minister and many politicians over the years. The word terrorist was liberally utilised by many politicians and quoted extensively in the media, again falling back on the rhetoric of the 'other' to generate fear within the broader community (Risso, 2019; Martin, 2019; Kelly, 2019). Instead of 'reds under the bed' (the term used during the McCarthy era to inspire unfounded fear of communists) this time it was the vegan terrorists waiting to disrupt daily lives, destroy livelihoods and violate the sanctity of the farming family home. In a notably excessive reaction, Australian Capital Territory Liberal Senator Zed Seselja allegedly referred 74 year-old vegan Pamela Collett to the Australian Federal Police for expressing her objection to his repeated use of the term vegan terrorist in debate over ag-gag (effectively gag) laws in federal parliament (Vegan Australia, 2019).

These responses are not to be wondered at as politicians have long appealed to populist rhetoric as a means to sow discord and apprehension amongst the voter base. The effect is to artificially construct public consent for the status quo. As Harvey states:

> Cultural and traditional values (such as belief in god and country or views of the position of women in society) and fear (of communists, immigrants, strangers, or 'others') can be mobilized to mask other realities. Political slogans can be invoked that mask specific strategies beneath vague rhetorical devices. (2005, p. 39)

By othering vegans and animal rights activists as un-Australian the prime minister pitched them against the hard-working farmers that Australia's national identity is constructed upon, playing into prevalent dole-bludger protestor rhetoric (activists don't have jobs, apparently). This not only undermines the actions of the protestors but further entrenches the demonisation of welfare-recipients, a handy two-for-one. The use of slogans to promote Australian cultural values also sought to protect agribusiness by further entrenching a national belief in meat. Maleovicky, Trémon and Zandonai state that politicians utilise slogans in this way as a means to promote the ethics of hard work and enterprise "in a bid to make otherwise socially and culturally divisive politics acceptable" (2018, p. 2). Barns (2019) notes that manufacturing fear of the other is a powerful tool that can be manipulated to exploit the vulnerabilities and insecurities of people within the community who feel confronted by the progress of change.

One would expect that the media reporting of protest actions and the political responses to those actions should at least remain impartial. However, concentrated media ownership by powerful individuals with corporate interests in animal exploitation as well government interference in the operations of the national broadcaster has undermined the integrity of the media to the extent that little to no reporting can be regarded as impartial. Rupert Murdoch (NewsCorp) owns the vast lamb, sheep and cattle producing property Cavan (Graham, 2019). In 2012 NewsCorp as a corporate entity invested $30 million in a number of cattle and chicken production facilities part-owned by a long time board member and failed to disclose the deal to investors (Edwards, 2012). In 2020 the Australian Senate agreed to commit to an inquiry into Murdoch's media ownership saturation and its impacts on democracy, following a petition campaign led by former prime minister Kevin Rudd that accrued over half a million signatures from the Australian public (Stayner, 2020). Kerry Stokes (Seven West Media) owns a vast cattle-ranching empire (Brammer, 2017). In 2017 he signed a sub-leasing deal subsuming two independent Aboriginal-owned properties into his holdings in the Kimberley, in what can be viewed as another example of economic and physical colonisation (Brammer, 2017). Former federal treasurer for the Howard Liberal National Party government and lawyer Peter Costello (CEO 9 Entertainment Co.) represented the National Farmers' Federation against the Australiasian Meat Industy Employees Union (AMIEU) in a number of abattoir wage cases in the 1980s (Costello, 1997).

The ABC, Australia's national broadcaster, has come under attack over the years for upholding liberal values. As Barns states:

> Monitoring the ABC is a full-time job for some in the Murdoch media as it pressures Canberra to take action against journalists and programs for pointing out human rights abuses or for giving a platform to despised elites such as the former human rights commissioner Gillian Triggs. (2019, p. 25)

In 2014 Triggs launched the National Enquiry into Children in Immigration Detention, an investigation into the health and well-being effects of detention experienced by refugee children held in mandatory detention (Borrello & Glenday, 2015). Government ministers under then prime minister Tony Abbott declared the government had lost confidence in her as president of the Australian Human Rights Commission (Borrello & Glenday, 2015). In 2017 conservative political commentator Chris Kenny penned a piece for the Murdoch-owned newspaper *The Australian* criticising Trigg's interview with ABC radio program Radio National. He claimed that the program "while funded to present objective and pluralistic news and views to the nation, has evolved into a de facto host broadcaster for the refugee lobby, climate alarmists, animal rights activists and general green left activism" (Kenny, 2017, n.p.).

Through the public record of the media, the government is able to manipulate public discourse in support of policies and legislation that undermine the foundations of democracy in Australia. The Hansard stands as an important document recording the attitudes and true intentions of government. By consistently promoting hatred for and fear of the other, state and federal governments have been able to justify the introduction of laws that affect every single individual inhabiting this continent. This has occurred without widespread opposition and has the effect of demonising those who engage in protest and restricting their ability to express political dissent. Thus new federal laws criminalising the posting of location information of farms were introduced without significant opposition (Kaye, 2019). The protestors themselves were not to blame for these political responses. Rather vegans and animal rights activists were scapegoated as a means to increase government control over the civic space, just as has been done over previous years with refugees, immigrants, and the Muslim community as the focus.

Whilst there was noted outcry by some politicians and members of the public as well as activists and organisations regarding the legislative measures implemented elsewhere, what has transpired in Tasmania has largely been overlooked by those beyond the borders of the island. Amendments to the failed 2014 anti-protest act (which were overturned by the High Court as unconstitutional), were introduced to parliament in November 2019 and eventually passed the lower house despite significant public opposition (Humphries, 2019; Maloney, 2019). The amendments currently await debate in the upper house where they are expected to be passed into legislation. They were described by Guy Barnett (minister for the Department of Primary Industry) as providing the country's "highest maximum penalty for the offence of trespassing while intentionally impeding business activity on business premises" (Appendix 2a). The proposed amendments and penalties are as follows:

- Trespass and property damage, maximum 21 years imprisonment;

- Separate offences for trespass with intent to impede business activity on the business premises including vehicles;

- Impediment of business causing economic loss subject to 18 months for a first offence and 4 years for a further offence;

- New summary offence of obstructing a public thoroughfare with the intention of impeding a business, including roads, pathways, overpasses, streets, water-ways, and public places;

- New offence for threats made with the intent to impede the carrying out of a business activity irrespective if the planned action eventuates;

- Provisions of the bill complement the Commonwealth incitement of trespass laws, such as using a mobile phone, and gives a broader range of circumstances and business to which they may apply;

- Removal of requirement for police to issue a move on order before initiating arrest. (Workplaces (Protection from Protestors) Amendment Act, 2019)

Under these laws, the only protests deemed legal are those that are issued permits by the state, under those circumstances dictated by the state. The state will not only criminalise the more extreme forms of protest such as facility occupations or lockdowns. The proposed bill will potentially criminalise slaughterhouse vigils, overpass banner drops, leafleting and campaigns targeting specific industries or businesses. The bill has been variously opposed by the Tasmanian Labor Party and by the Tasmanian Greens, with O'Connor labelling the proposed amendments a "bill of rights for business" (Appendix 2c). Her claims were all but confirmed by the then Liberal premier Will Hodgman:

It is a bill that is supported by, amongst others, the TFGA, the TCCI [The Tasmanian Chamber of

Commerce and Industry], FIAT [Forest Industry Association of Tasmania] the Tasmanian Minerals, Manufacturing & Energy Council, the Tasmanian Seafood Industry Council, and the Tasmanian Small Business Council. That is who we will be standing alongside, and standing up for today, with respect to this legislation. (Tasmanian Government, 2019, Appendix 2b)

The then premier only referenced industry lobby groups in his speech on the bill and Barnett only made vague reference to the 400 submissions on the bill listed on the Department of Justice website. What both politicians failed to address was that of the submissions provided during community consultation by individuals, advocacy groups and industry proponents, only two were in support of the bill, being the Tasmanian Minerals, Manufacturing & Energy Council and a member of the public (O'Connor, 2019, Appendix 2c). The bill does not have widespread public support, yet is predicted to be passed by the Legislative Council irrespective of the concerns of the broader population.

The anti-democratic sentiment at the heart of this bill is cause enough for concern alone. Its proponents are conspicuously placing demands of industry above the cornerstones of engagement with democratic processes through dissent. To the extent that the government seeks to criminalise even the most benign expressions of protests, is deeply problematic. It shows a commitment to the continuation of the carceral state in pursuit of facilitating the demands of industry (see the third essay for further discussion of the carceral state and its connections with animal exploitation). The Tasmanian Liberal government is investing $270 million in the contentious Northern Regional Prison Project due for completion within the next ten years (Archer, 2019). This is evidence of the government's continued commitment to carceral methods of social control as opposed to investment in social programs that could limit or eliminate the need for physical prisons. Also of grave concern, the Tasmanian Liberal government has sent the photo identification information of over 400 000 Tasmanians to the federal government's national facial biometrics matching database without prior consent, information that may be accessed and utilised by agencies authorised by the federal government (Holmes, 2019). And if that were not enough, extra surveillance cameras are to be installed on parliament lawns, the one place Tasmanians may be legally permitted to congregate in protest once the anti-protest laws are enacted (Killick, 2020). The cameras supplier HikVision is also the chosen supplier of the Chinese government, providing surveillance technology throughout occupied Tibet and in Xinjiang where the oppression, incarceration and murder of Uighur Muslims by the State continues unchecked (Killick, 2020).

When government fulfils its obligations to industry, creating the environments necessary for the establishment of markets and the maximisation of profits, the full expression of the democratic process must by necessity be impinged upon, to the detriment of civic rights. Australia is claimed to be a liberal democracy, a nation supposedly built upon the ideals of tolerance and fairness, upon diversity of beliefs and cultures, and upon freedom of thought and action (Barns, 2019). However, the growing power of industry lobby groups and their influence on public policy, including the public education system, at the expense of the Australian taxpayer, undermines these very ideals. Indeed, the channeling of tax dollars into supporting private enterprise can be viewed as an enclosure of the commons of public funds. The power of these lobby groups is inextricably connected with a media that is owned and operated by those with a vested interest in the continuation of industrialised animal exploitation and that is used by the government to malign dissent and entrench a nationalism built upon a colonial mythology. Thus, classrooms become potential labour and consumer markets, and taxpayer dollars are used to prop up private industry irrespective of our ethical ideals. The citizen's ability to engage in political dissent becomes restricted by laws designed to the benefit of private industries and corporate interests. Thus, the individual ceases to live in a liberal democracy and becomes little more than units of production or consumption. The animal industrial complex, like all other industrial complexes, is eroding democracy. Under such a system how can we claim to have freedom of thought or action? The simple act of purchasing a carton of cow's milk or a package of lamb's flesh ceases to be engagement with free consumer choice. It is instead a decision the individual has been manipulated towards by the lobby groups and the government via public institutions and the media, though we may not realise it. There is no consent under this mode of consumption. Not least of all with regards to the innumerable other animals whose consent is fundamentally violated within this system of exploitation.

The connections between government and the myriad other industrial complexes that constitute the web, such as the media industrial complex, the military industrial complex, the prison industrial complex, and of course the animal industrial complex, are intricate and complicated. Each supports the other through a network of businesses, politicians and powerful individuals who are prepared to interfere in the democratic process, even to the point of violence in some cases. The complexities of this web therefore require the animal advocate to understand where the individual strands of the web are positioned and what support they may lend and attempt to pull those threads in order to collapse the web. A singular apolitical 'go vegan' message that does not take into consideration the complexes that govern our lives and have the power to undermine our civic freedoms cannot hope to deconstruct the systems and networks of the animal industrial complex. As such we must not simply define our focus as advocates; we must also understand the myriad complexities that constitute the scope of our advocacy. For as the American writer, feminist and civil rights activist Lorde so famously said: "There is no thing as a single-issue struggle because we do not live single-issue lives" (2007, p. 138).

References

AgriFutures Australia (2019). *Annual report 2018-19*. https://www.agrifutures.com.au/product/agrifutures-australia-annual-report-2018-19/

Archer, E. (2019). *A northern prison for Tasmania's future*. https://www.examiner.com.au/story/6411516/a-northern-prison-for-tasmanias-future

Australian Bureau of Statistics (ABS) (2018). *Household income and wealth, Australia 2017-18*. https://www.abs.gov.au/statistics/economy/finance/household-income-and-wealth-australia/latest-release

Australian Eggs Ltd (2019). *Annual report 2018-19*. https://www.australianeggs.org.au/who-we-are/annual-reports

Australian Meat Processors Corporation (2019). *Annual report 2018-19*. https://www.ampc.com. au/about/corporate-reports

Australian Parliament House (2020). *Hansard*. www.aph. gov.au/hansard

Australian Pork (2019). *Annual report 2018-19*. https://www. australianpork.com.au/library-resources/publications/annual-reports/

Bajkowski, J. (2019). *Robodebt collector owned by company being sued by ACCC*. https://www.itnews.com.au/news/robodebts-collection-agency-owned-by-company-being-Sued-by-accc-531368

Baker-Dowdell, J. (2017). *Biosecurity improved in Tasmania with Powranna truck wash*. https://www.examiner.com.au/story/5109663/powrannas-truck-wash-scheduled-for-april-2018-opening/

Barcan, A. (1998). *Radical students: The old left at Sydney University* (First Edition). Melbourne University Publishers.

Barnett, G. (2020). *New CEO for RSPCA Tasmania*. https://www.premier.tas.gov.au/releases/new_ceo_for_rspca_tasmania

Barns, G. (2019). *The rise of the right: The war on Australian liberal values*. Hardie Grant Books.

Best, S. (2011). Introduction: Pathologies of power and the rise of the global industrial complex. In S. Best, R. Kahn, A. J. Nocella, & P. McClaren (Eds.), *The global industrial complex: Systems of domination* (pp. ix-xxv). Lexington Books.

Borrello, E., & Glenday, J. (2015) *Gillian Triggs: Tony Abbott says government has lost confidence in Human Rights Commission president*. https://www.abc.net.au/news/2015-02-24/gillian-triggs-says-brandis-wants-her-to-quit-rights-commission/6247520?nw=0

Brammer, J. (2017). *Kerry Stokes seeks beef stake with Kimberley station sublease plan*. https://thewest.com.au/business/agriculture/kerry-stokes-seeks-beef-stake-with-kimberley-station-sublease-plan-ng-b88615145z

Breunig, C. (1977). *The age of revolution and reaction, 1789-1850*. (2nd Ed.). W. W. Norton & Co.

Costello, P. (1997). *Address to the National Farmers' Federation Conference, Rydges Eagle Hawk, Canberra*. https://ministers. treasury.gov.au/ministers/peter-costello-1996/speeches/ address-national-farmers-federation-conference-rydges-eagle

Dairy Australia (2019). *Annual report 2018-19*. https://www. dairyaustralia.com.au/resource-repository/2020/07/09/ dairy-australia-annual-report-201819#.X8MZi3k7YwA

Eaglehawk, W. (2020). Species justice is for every body. In D. Ross, M. Brueckner, M. Palmer & W. Eaglehawk (Eds.), *Eco-activism and social work: New directions in leadership and group work* (pp. 100-110). Routledge.

Edwards, J. (2012). *Why News Corp. invested $30 million in cow and chicken farms*. https://www.businessinsider.com/ news-corp-invested-30-million-in-farms-2012-12

Ferguson, M., & Barnett, G. (2020). *We're keeping Tasmanian pork on your fork*. https://www.premier.tas.gov.au/mersey_emergency_ department_to_reopen_247/covid_safety_ plans_crucial_for_businesses_moving_forward/ were_keeping_tasmanian_pork_on_your_fork

Fisher, A. (2019). *The ban on live sheep exports has just been lifted. Here's what's changed*. https://theconversation.com/ the-ban-on-live-sheep-exports-has-just-been-lifted-heres- whats-changed-123998

Fisheries Research & Development Corporation (2019). *Annual report 2018-19*. https://www. frdc.com.au/ about/corporate-documents/annual-reports

Fraser, G., Knutsen, S., Sirirat, R., Maschak, A., Orlich, M., & Jaceldo-Siegl, K. (2020). Dairy, soy, and the risk of breast cancer: those confounded milks. *International Journal of Epidemiology, dya007,* DOI: 10.1093/ije/dyaa007

Graham, V. (2019). *Cavan Station takes a data dive into grazing success.* https://www.farmonline.com.au/story/6534331/ data-driven-grazing-mangement-a-winner-at-cavan-station/

Graves, L. (2012). *Sofia Gatica, Argentine activist, faced anonymous death threats for fighting Monsanto herbicide.* https://www.huffpost. com/entry/argentine-activist-sofia-gatica-Monsanto_n_1475659

Greenville, J. (2020). *Analysis of government support for Australian agricultreseauralproducers.* https://www.agriculture.gov.au/abares/ rch-topics/trade/analysis-of-government-support- agricultural-producers

Hardy, E. (2019). *Curious compassionate conservatism. Who will benefit from the government's welfare reform?* https://www. themonthly.com.au/today/elle-hardy/2019/09/2019/1568008047/ curious-compassionate-conservatism

Harvey, D. (2005). *A brief history of neoliberalism.* Oxford University Press.

Heaney, C. (2019). *Cashless welfare card could unfairly target thousands of Aboriginal People in the NT, Senate committee hears.* https://www.abc.net.au/news/2019-11-01/cashless- welfare-card-committee-hearing-northern-territory/11662892

Hettiarachchi, K., & Deane, R. (2019). *Milky dream turns sour farmers*. http://www.sundaytimes.lk/190224/news/milky-dream-turns-sour-farmers-337867.html

Holmes, A. (2019). *Government stands firm on sending 410,000 Tasmanian licence photos to facial recognition database*. https://www.examiner.com.au/story/6554372/government-stands-firm-on-sending-licence-photos-to-database/

Hosier, P., & Coulter, E. (2018). *Devonport abattoir closure puts more than 100 Tasmanian jobs at risk*. https://www.abc.net.au/news/2018-10-22/devonport-abattoir-closure-puts-tasmanian-jobs-at-risk/10406180

Humphries, A. (2019). *Move to revive anti-protest laws in Tasmanian a 'face-saving exercise', Bob Brown says*. https://www.abc.net.au/news/2019-01-28/tasmania-revives-anti-protest-laws/10755796

Kaye, B. (2019). *Australia PM seeks new law to penalize animal rights activists*. https://www.reuters.com/article/us-australia-protests-vegans-idUSKCN1RM0ZG

Kelly, F. (2019). *When does activism turn into terrorism? National Farmers' Federation slams animal rights group*. https://www.abc.net.au/radionational/programs/breakfast/when-does-activism-turn-into-terrorism/10734448

Kenny, C. (2017). *ABC fails to learn lessons from Triggs*. https://www.theaustralian.com.au/business/media/abc-fails-to-learn-lessons-from-triggs

Killick, D. (2020). *Concern over Chinese 'spy' camera near parliament*. https://www.themercury.com.au/news/politics/

concern-over-chinese-spy-cameras-near-parliament/news-story/c39e9aadb287f68d022861fd33f95954

Knowles, L., & Heanue, S. (2019). *Australian cattle exported to Sri Lanka dying and malnourished, local farmers left suicidal.* https://www/abc.net.au/news/2019-04-04/australian-dairy-cattle-sent-to-sri-lanka-dying-malnourished/10936258

Lorde, A. (2007). Learning from the 60s. In. A. Lorde (Ed.), *Sister outsider: Essays & speeches* (pp. 134-44). The Crossing Press.

Maleovicky, N., Trémon, A., & Zandonai, S. (2018). Slogans: Circulations, contestations, and current engagements with neo-liberal policies. In. N. Maleovicky, A. Trémon & S. Zandonai (Eds.), *Slogans: Subjection, subversion, and the politics of neoliberalism* (pp. 1-23). Routledge.

Maloney, M. (2019). *Tasmania's House of Assembly passes country's toughest anti-protest laws.* https://www.examiner.com.au/story/6517184/anti-protest-laws-pass-the-house-of-assembly/

Martin, S. (2019). *Animal activist group that publishes farm details for protests has charity status revoked.* https://www.theguardian.com/australia-news/2019/nov/18/animal-activist-group-that-publishes-farm-details-for-protests-has-charity-status-revoked

McCulloch, D. (2019). *Prime minister admonishes animal activists.* https://www.canberratimes.com.au/story/6006111/prime-minister-admonishes-animal-activists

McIlroy, J. (2020). *Cashless welfare card entrenches racism, poverty, corruption.* https://www.greenleft.org.au/content/cashless-welfare-card-entrenches-racism-poverty-corruption

McCormack, M. (2020). *Transcript: Northern Cooperative Meat Company Press Conference, 11 September 2020*. https://www.michaelmccormack.com.au/media-releases/2020/9/11/transcript-northern-co-operative-meat-company-press-conference-11-september-2020

Meat & Livestock Australia MLA (2019). *Annual report 2018-19*. https://www.mla.com.au/about-mla/how-we-are-governed/Planning-reporting/annual-reporting/annual-report-2018-19/

Morris, R. (2019). *Tasmanian Quality Meats gains funding commitment for major expansions*. https://www.theadvocate.com.au/story/6115153/election-commitment-a-saviour-for-states-meat-processing

Morrison, O. (2020). *Ditch soy alternatives for cows' milk says the Sustainable Food Trust*. https://www.foodnavigator.com/Article/2020/08/13/Ditch-soy-alternatives-for-cows-milk-says-the-Sustainable-Food-Trust

Murphy, S. (2019). *Vegans vow to rage against the farming machine*. https://www.abc.net.au/news/2019-05-30/vegan-activists-vow-to-rage-against-the-farming-machine/11145650

News First (2020). *Sajith urges govt. to suspend dairy heifer imports*. https://www.newsfirst.lk/2020/05/28/Sajith-urges-govt-to-suspend-dairy-heifer-imports

Nibert, D. (2011). Origins and consequences of the animal industrial complex. In S. Best, R. Kahn, A. J. Nocella, & P. McLaren (Eds.), *The global industrial complex: Systems of domination* (pp. 197-209). Lexington Books.

Noske, B. (1997). *Beyond boundaries. Humans and animals* (revised ed.). Black Rose Books.

Observatory of Economic Complexity (OEC) (2018). *Where does Australia import soy from?* https://oec.world/en/visualize/tree_map/hs92/import/aus/show/42304/2018

O'Connor, C. (2020). *Treasury-Exclusive Brethren*. https://tasmps.green.org.au/parliament/treasury-exclusive-brethren

Perpitch, N., & Weber, D. (2018). *Former live export manager avoids jail over role in 22,000 sheep deaths in Pakistan*. https://www.abc.net.au/news/2018-05-22/former-live-export-boss-avoids-jail-over-role-in-sheep-deaths/9786208

Powell, M. (2020). *Cheap salmon farm fees costing state billions of dollars, Tasmanian Alliance for Marine Protection claims*. https://www/theadvocate.com.au/6890440/cheap-salmon-farm-fees-costing-tasmanians-billions-group-claims

Risso, A. (2019). *NSW Deputy repeats 'farm terrorists' label*. https://www.canberratimes.com.au/story/6384025/nsw-deputy-repeats-farm-terrorists-label/

Rockliffe, J. (2016). *Funding secured for Powranna truck wash*. http://www.premier.tas.gov.au/releases/funding_secured_for_powranna_truck_wash

Sheep Central (2020). *Western Australia to get 20,000-head sheep feedlot*. https://www.sheepcentral.com/western-queensland-to-get-20000-head-capacity-sheep-feedlot/

Shiva, V. (2011). The agricultural industrial complex. In
S. Best, R. Kahn, A. J. Nocella, & P. McClaren (Eds.),
The industrial global complex: Systems of domination
(pp. 169-195). Lexington Books.

Stayner, T. (2020). *Senate votes to hold media diversity inquiry
after record breaking murdoch petition.* https://www.sbs.com.
au/news/senate-votes-to-hold-media-diversity-inquiry-after-
record-breaking-murdoch-petition

Storrs, L. (2015). *McCarthyism and the second red scare.*
https://oxfordre.com/american history/view/10.1093/
acrefore/9780199329175.001.0001/acrefore-9780199329175-e-6

Sustainable Food Trust (2020). *About us.* https://www.
sustainablefoodtrust.org/about-us/

Tasmanian Agricultural Productivity Group (TAPG) (2020).
TAPG: About us. https://www/tapg.net/about-us/

Tasmanian Farmers & Graziers Association (TFGA) (2020).
Fighting for Tasmanian farmers. https://tfga.com.au/about-us

Tasmanian Freight Equalisation Scheme (2020). *Overview.*
https://www.infrastructure.gov.au/maritime/tasmanian-
transport-schemes/tasmanian/

Tasmanian Government (2019). *Hansard 27/11/2019.*
See Appendix 2b.

Twine, R. (2012). Revealing the 'animal-industrial
complex': A concept and method for critical animal studies.
Journal for critical animal studies, 10(1), 12-39.

Twomey, S. (2014). *Wimmera secures more jobs through Luv-a-Duck expansion*. https://www.weeklytimesnow.com.au/agribusiness/wimmera-secures-more-jobs-through-luvaduck-expansion/news-story/2b62f33ac25088b52c7755d2dd96617b

Vegan Australia (2019). *74 year old vegan outraged for being reported to Australian Federal Police*. https://www.veganaustralia.org.au/74_year_old_vegan_outraged_for_being_ Reported_to_police

Wahlquist, C. (2019). *Live exporter charged with sheep cruelty over deadly Awassi shipment*. https://www.theguardian.com/australia-news/2019/jul/31/live-exporter-charged-with-sheep-cruelty-over-deadly-awassi-shipment

Wilkins, K. (2018). *JBS and Tasmanian Quality Meats negotiating for pork agreement*. https://www.examiner.com.au/story/5737310/jbs-and-tasmanian-quality-meats-negotiating-for-pork-agreement

Wilson, J. (2020). *Religious profit: Expanding the cashless welfare card ties in with Morrison's beliefs*. https://theaimn.com/religious-profit-expanding-the-cashless-welfare-card-ties-in-with morrison's-beliefs

Wolloch, I. (1982). *Eighteenth-century Europe: Tradition and progress, 1715-1789*. W. W. Norton & Co.

Woods, H. (2020). *How billionaires saw their net worth increase by half a trillion dollars during the pandemic*. https://www.businessinsider.com/billionaires-net-worth-increases-coronavirus-Pandemic-2020-07

Workabout Australia (2012). *Successful project grants under the Tasmanian government innovation and investment fund.* https://workaboutaustralia.worldsecuresystems.com/ announcements/successful-project-grants-under-the-tasmanian-government-innovation-and-investment-fund

Tasmanian Government (2019). *Workplaces (Protection from Protesters) Amendment Act 2019: Act No. of 2019.* https:// www.justice.tas.gov.au/community-consultation/closed-community-consultations2/workplaces-protection-from-protesters-amendment-bill2019

Young, E. (2020). *Backlash after senate inquiry recommends expansion of controversial cashless welfare card.* https://www. sbs.com.au/v1/news/article/backlash-after-senate-inquiry-reco mmends-expansion-of-controversial-cashless-welfare-card/ e1027eac-9b0b-4a14-b9c0-e081cab9d8b8

'Animals only' ideology and the scope of the vegan movement

The vegan movement is largely defined by and dedicated to the animal rights movement, although not all who advocate for other animals are vegan. For example, I was a dog rescuer and foster carer before I was a vegan. At the same time the vegan movement is deeply divided. This division is centred upon different views with regard to the interconnected issues of justice and thereby, of the systems of oppression that affect humans, other animals and non-animal entities within and without societies. Many members of the vegan community have chosen to align themselves with an 'animals only' ideology. This ideology seeks to exclude consideration for human rights from within animal advocacy. The argument is that to include human rights dilutes the message of veganism and animal liberation, causing other animals to become sidelined within their own movement. However, such an exclusionary stance may prevent the creation of networks with other human communities that could facilitate animal liberation. Some have taken the 'animals only' ideology to its extreme conclusion, anchoring their messaging in profound misanthropy to the point of eco-fascism. Misanthropy refers to dislike of or prejudice against humans (Bloch & Ferguson, 1989/2020). Eco-fascism extends on misanthropy in its call for racial purity as the preferred human identity (Taylor & Zimmerman, 2008) and ties this to protection of Earth at any cost (Manavis, 2018). However, what some vegans and organisations may fail to comprehend is the difference between focus and scope. It is my aim in this essay to work through these myriad issues and define the focus and the scope of veganism which is inclusive of, and prioritises, animal rights while at the same time being a broader justice movement.

Before defining the scope and focus of veganism, I will investigate what veganism is and what it has the potential to be. This was addressed briefly in the introduction, where veganism was defined as an ethical stance against the exploitation of other animals as far as is practicable. As Brueck states:

> Veganism is not a diet. Interchanging *vegan* with *plant-based* is speciesist, as it focuses on "food animals" while ignoring those used for clothing, entertainment, testing, and all other forms of exploitation. It also equates plant-based products produced via

exploitative labor practices with those produced in most just ways. This further reduces our movement to one that only exists for some species. (2017, p. 6)

Prioritising humans' interests over other animals and the exploitation of some animals is inherently discriminatory and speciesist. The concept of speciesism was defined by Ryder in 1970, who argued that as animals other than humans exist on the same physical continuum as humans then by right they should be given equal moral consideration (Ryder, 2010). It is this idea of moral consideration that has formed the foundational belief of the abolitionist position that veganism is not simply a consumer behaviour but rather a *moral imperative* (Francione, 2016). This ethical position rejects the exclusion of other animals from moral consideration within human society. However, just as vegan is not interchangeable with plant-based, nor is veganism interchangeable with anti-speciesism. In denying other animals' agency (Taylor, 2013) by describing them as 'helpless' or 'voiceless' many vegans still engage in speciesist behaviours and dialogue. This occurs by relying on distinctly ableist and humanist tropes, as well as words such as it to describe other animals, thus relating them to inanimate objects rather than recognising them as sentient beings (Haraway, 2008).

Veganism needs to include anti-speciesism to alter the ways in which human society interacts with and regards other animals and to pursue just outcomes for other animals. It is not simply a matter of refraining from eating and using other animals, though this matters. It is a matter of recreating entire systems and societies that currently situate humans as holding a place of dominance over life on Earth by right of species alone. This superiority complex is dependent upon the *misothery* of animals who are not humans. Misothery is a term coined by Mason (2005) that refers to a hatred or contempt for animals and, by extension, the natural world. Thus, being an animal renders one inferior to being human. Håkansson states the challenge in the following way:

> By remembering that we are not unique in our life, our sentience, or our capacity to feel and think, we can revolutionise what social justice means, and who it helps. Simply put, without speciesism, everyone in the realm of social justice could remove their barrier of concern and include all animals. Those we destroy the native habitat of, those we farm and slaughter, those we are. (2020, n.p.)

The adoption of anti-speciesism as the framework for veganism, positions veganism as a socio-political movement striving to attain social justice for other animals (and humans) rather than as a consumer behaviour. Thus, veganism becomes a reimagining of the social space that currently confines whilst it simultaneously excludes other animals. However, this does not necessitate the decentering of other animals from within their own movement. Animal advocates can deconstruct misothery and embrace the liberatory potential of veganism within a collective context by understanding the concepts of focus and scope.

Every social justice movement has a focus. Whether it be anti-racism, feminism, the anti-war movement, or environmentalism. Each movement works alongside one another in pursuit of justice for their specific cause. The focus of each is the predetermined result towards which the primary efforts of those engaged within that space are directed. The predetermined result of veganism working within a social justice context is the liberation of other animals from human exploitation. The focus provides the framework that informs the actions, dialogues, relationships and labour that is undertaken. However, the scope is the entirety of those actions, dialogues and labour, as well as the outcomes and benefits that are realised, both primary and secondary. This encompasses the many ways in which animal advocates engage with society and the connections made with other individuals and spaces, as well as the improvements to society that can result from the realisation of that primary focus. Cross, one of the founders of the vegan movement, states:

> Its official definition — "the doctrine that [hu]man[s] should live without exploiting animals" — is accurate, precise and comprehensive, but not always fully understood. This is not as surprising as it might seem, for so rarely have nine short words enshrined a reform so massive, the achievement of which would bring a new world and new [...] [humans] to inhabit it. (1954, p. 9)

Neither Leslie Cross nor Donald Watson, another co-founder of the movement, invented veganism. Veganism has been central to many cultural groups across the globe as a facet of their belief systems and relationships with the natural world and each other. Jainism, as one example, is an ancient Indian religion where the adherents promote a way of living that rejects violence against humans, other animals and the natural world (National Geographic, 2020). The practice of nonviolence is understood to be the way to overcome the cycle of rebirths through the adoption of a spiritual and ethical life. Veganism features amongst many communities of Jains, though not all Jains are exclusively vegan. The efforts of the early vegan society as founders of a liberatory movement were focused on creating an accessible definition of veganism for what was then the modern era. The works written by Cross (1954), Watson (1944) and their colleagues show that veganism was not created to the exclusion of humans, rather that it was for the inclusion of other animals within the moral consideration of human society (Batt, 1964). To that end, the most expansive definition of veganism has been synonymous with the ideal of collective liberation.

The interlinked rise of the animal industrial complex and neoliberalism as a dominant political ideology has resulted in the deepening of social and ecological crises. Additionally the numbers of other animals slaughtered appears to be increasing (Animal Charity Evaluators, 2018). This has brought the vegan movement to a crossroad. A limited focus on vegan consumerism as animal rights advocacy hides the associated issues relating to worker exploitation, environmental degradation and corporate expansion. It becomes imperative that animal advocates engage in a dialogue to adapt the original definitions of veganism and potentially create new ones in their place. However, the dialogue is currently dominated by a handful of populist icons and organisations and their creation of quick-consume apolitical online content. To date, this has taken precedence over critical analysis and the nonviolent ethico-political positioning of the vegan movement. Economics and politics are neither sexy nor easy to understand and are therefore less readily consumable. Nevertheless, people do value justice, peace and wellbeing. Veganism provides practicable ethics, language and ways forward that are inclusive of all sentient beings, non-animal entities and the planet.

It is not divisive to question the ethics of veganism, the animal rights movement and its proponents. Rather, questioning and criticism are essential facets of the movement's ethical, social and political evolution. This will enable the commitment to grow beyond individual consumer choices towards the realisation of liberation. According to Best:

> Certainly, individuals need to take responsibility for their choices and the consequences of their actions, such as by engaging the ecological and ethical imperative to become vegan. However, it is also crucial to recognize the formidable power of corporations, the state, mass media, schools, and other institutions in people's lives, and to appreciate the constraints imposed by poverty, class, and social conditioning. (2014, p. 44)

Corporations whose wealth is generated from the exploitation of other animals understand the power of money and how to wield it to devastating effect. In 2020 popular oat-milk brand Oatly sold a stake of the company to investment corporation Blackstone for $200 million (Helmore, 2020). Blackstone has been directly linked to deforestation in the Amazon as well as the company's owner donating directly to support Donald Trump's regime (Oguh, 2020). The deal was met with wide condemnation within the vegan and animal rights community. It caused damage to Oatly's carefully crafted public image as a trendy and sustainable alternative to dairy (Helmore, 2020). Unilever (2020) has announced a new global sales target of $1.6 billion from plant-based meats and dairy alternatives, including the acquisition of numerous vegan companies. In November 2020 an Associated Press investigation into the palm oil industry exposed worker exploitation and human trafficking involved in the harvesting of fruit that enters the supply chain of multinational corporations including Unilever (Mason & McDowell, 2020). At the same time, Amnesty International (2020) exposed the business partnership between Kirin Holdings and Myanma Economic Holdings (MEHL), with Myanmar's military receiving massive revenue from its investment in MEHL. Thus funding their military operations which have been shown to include war crimes and serious human rights abuses. Kirin is the parent company of Lion Pty Ltd. who owns a number of Australian brands including the popular milk alternative brand Vitasoy (Amnesty International, 2020).

These deals are examples of why the vegan movement simply cannot afford to restrict itself to an apolitical definition of veganism. Corporations whose ethos directly opposes the fundamental ideals of veganism are able to insert themselves into the process and turn it to their advantage. The question becomes, what or whom are animal advocates prepared to sacrifice in the pursuit of access to plant-based products? As such the scope of the movement should (among other things) include "theorizing the interconnections between the A-IC [animal industrial complex] and other sectors of the global economy" (Twine, 2012, p. 16).

As discussed in the first essay, the justice struggle needs to be against myriad industrial complexes, webs of political, corporate and social institutions. These powerful entities support one another irrespective of how many plant-based options are available in a supermarket, or how many vegan cafes are established. Humans cannot consume their way to liberation. Liberation for human and other animals is inextricably entwined such that humans must rather pull at the threads that keep the industrial complex web firmly anchored. It is not contested that the realisation of the liberation of other animals would primarily benefit other animals. However, within the scope of that realisation lie benefits to human communities also.

The closure of concentrated animal feeding operations including feedlots and fish feedlots, as well the slaughterhouses both connected to the facilities or situated some distance away, would not only result in an end to industrialised animal flesh production. Their closures would also result in safer living conditions for those communities forced to live in close proximity which are impacted by the smells, the pollution of water sources and the disposal of waste from these facilities. Animal agriculture has been reported as a significant contributor to the climate crisis with the United Nations (UN) predicting that the increasing global appetite for flesh is a significant contributing factor in the ongoing climate crisis (Lymery & Oakeshott, 2014). The dismantling of industrial animal production systems could thus be a crucial strategy in combating climate change which would benefit human health and survival along with that of other animals in the natural world.

The increasingly intensified model of animal farming to maximise corporate profits requires a commensurate overuse of antibiotics (Centers for Disease Control and Prevention (CDPC), 2019). There is a lack of realisation that animal liberation would assist in combating the evolution of antibiotic resistant pathogens that pose a very real risk to human health in the here and now. The CDCP in the foreword of their 2019 report on antibiotic overuse state that people should "stop referring to a coming post-antibiotic era — it's already here" (2019, p. vi). They are calling attention to the decreasing effectiveness of antibiotics in agriculture whereby other animal diseases can cross over and impact human health. The majority of these zoonotic diseases have originated as a result of the dysfunctional human relationship with other animals such that their liberation could assist in potentially preventing future pandemics (CDCP, 2017). The global crisis created by COVID-19 has given rise to extensive discussions regarding wet markets and CAFOs (Standaert, 2020; Foer & Gross, 2020). There has been very little discussion of the adoption of veganism (as both ideal and practicable) and the dismantling of animal farming systems as a means to prevent future pandemics.

The apparent environmental, health and social benefits of human animal liberation fall within the scope of the movement without detracting from the primary focus. Indeed, reaching out to the human communities most impacted by the social and ecological effects of animal exploitation can result in positive outcomes in preventing the expansion or creation of new facilities. For example, there was a successful campaign to prevent the construction of a new pig farm in Blantyre in 2017. After a collaborative effort between animal rights activists and community groups, the local council had no option but to reject the application to build a 25 000-animal piggery in the area (Doherty & Shields, 2017).

All too often, animal advocates rely upon comparisons between systems of oppression as a tool in their public or online outreach activism without actively engaging with other social justice spaces. This tends to occur without seeking to understand the complexities and nuances, or even the lived experiences of those individuals and communities most affected by social injustice. According to Opotow:

> [...] a critical understanding of social justice must be attentive to the nuances and complications along the inclusionary/exclusionary continuum where tension between justice and injustice can yield partial, transitory, illusory or faux inclusion. (2018, p. 53)

Relying on analogies and imagery drawing from the lived experiences of other oppressed communities without a working understanding of those experiences (and a commitment to addressing those injustices) may make one's advocacy appear to be inclusive. However, that inclusivity is superficial as it does nothing to deconstruct those systems of oppression that are used as analogy. As Ko states:

> [...] those who are most eager to juxtapose these kinds of images or discuss how animal slavery is relevantly "like" human (black) slavery many times are the same people who tend to be dismissive of or resistant to views in which animal oppression and human oppression are *thought about together* and *in the same spaces* with the aim of taking to task racism, sexism, speciesism, ableism, and so on — or coloniality in general — *in tandem*. (2016, p. 84)

Without an understanding of social justice issues of the communities animal advocates operate within, including those of other animals, they may instead position themselves as the focus of the movement. This can reinforce oppression, when, as the self-appointed spokespeople for other animals (and humans) it excludes the voices, experiences and lives of those whom they claim to represent. Animal advocates can effectively other other animals, undermining their autonomy whilst they, as the 'saviours' determine how other animals are to be treated by society without including them within society itself (Braidotti, 2013). Too often other animals are effectively scapegoated in order to excuse white supremacy, transphobia, misogyny, ableism, and classism within a movement supposedly dedicated to the pursuit of justice. Animals only ideology in the vegan movement excludes not only other humans from participating, but other animals as well.

This, of course, is only applicable if an individual or group views the vegan and animal rights movement as belonging within the social justice sphere, or if they believe in the validity of social justice itself. Certainly there appears to be significant hostility directed by those who promote animals only ideology towards those whose advocacy is informed by the principles of intersectionality. However, if one does not view animal rights as a social justice movement, then where do animal rights belong? As Donaldson & Kymlicka state:

> We are part of a shared society with innumerable animals, one which would continue to exist even if we eliminated cases of forced participation. It is simply not tenable for ART [animal rights theory] to assume that humans can inhabit a separate realm from other animals in which interaction, and potential conflict, could largely be eliminated. Ongoing

> interaction is inevitable, and this reality must lie at the
> centre of animal rights, not be swept to the periphery.
> (2011, p. 8)

Even after every slaughterhouse, feedlot, or vivisection laboratory is closed down, we will still share spaces and societies with other animals and must develop the strategies necessary to make that co-existence as harmonious as possible. An isolationist approach that seeks to remove humans from the company of other animals is physically and socially impossible unless we pursue a policy of self-extermination. Views such as 'humans are the virus' or support for population control as a means to combat increasing environmental degradation (and the associated impacts on other animals) are frequently promoted by misanthropic vegans and animal rights activists who themselves may claim not to support ideologies that lead to the marginalisation of other human communities. However, given the structural power imbalances in society, these views can easily become aligned with eco-fascism and place vulnerable and marginalised communities in jeopardy.

Eco-fascism is a fundamentally conservative ideology that ostensibly places the needs of the Earth above the rights of human communities. However, it can belie a dangerous ethics as Taylor & Zimmerman state:

> Eco-fascism in its most extreme form links the racial
> purity of a people to the well-being of the nation's
> land; calls for the removal or killing of native peoples;

and may also justify profound individual and collective sacrifice of its own people for the health of the natural environment. (2008, p. 458)

The fetishisation of the purity of blood and linking human identity indelibly to the land form the fundamental ideology of eco-fascism. Eco-fascism was previously manifested in the Nazi ideology of "Blut und Boden" or blood and soil (Manavis, 2018). Eco-fascism recently reared its head mid-2020 upon the release of former Animal Liberation Front (ALF) activist Walter Bond from prison, whereupon he co-released a website *Vegan Final Solution* (Anarchists Worldwide, 2020). The site actively dog-whistled Nazism through the name of the site, the motifs and imagery utilised, whilst also advocating for the killing of non-vegans and the restricting of human breeding exclusively to vegan activists (Anarchists Worldwide, 2020). The website was pulled shortly after launching (NonZeroSum, 2020). Purity of blood and purity of community are integrally fascist ideologies. This is not to say that all proponents of animals only ideology are themselves eco-fascists. However, misanthropy to the extent that humans deny the socio-political progress necessary for the wellbeing and survival of other marginalised human communities based purely on their belonging to the human species skirts dangerously close to eco-fascist ideology and as such should come under very careful scrutiny.

There has been considerable discussion regarding the application of intersectionality within veganism and the animal rights movement. Some have adopted the label of 'intersectional vegan' as an identity whilst others have labelled the concept a cancer and its proponents human supremacists. Intersectionality was defined by Crenshaw (1989) as a framework to explore the experiences of Black and Brown femmes in society and the intersections of the oppressive systems within which they operate and against which they strive. In later years the concept has been expanded to cover the intersections of all oppressions within society, including (but not limited to) race, gender, sexuality, class, social opportunity, religion, nationality, and body type (Watts, 2015). The adoption (or appropriation in some cases) of intersectionality as a framework for veganism and animal rights has been performed with limited critical analysis by many vegans who have assumed the concept as a marker of identity. As Sebastian states "intersectional feminism belongs to black and brown femmes" (2017a, n.p). He also states that animals deserve a movement of their own. Intersectionality as a concept was not designed to include species other than human and, therefore, as a framework may not be well suited to veganism. As Kassam attests from her personal experiences:

> I am also part of some pro-intersectional groups [...]. They have really helped me become aware of some of my own privileges and unconscious biases. I still have a long way to go, and I expect this will be a lifelong process, but I have noticed that, while people are regularly called out for racist, sexist, ableist, and other types of oppressive language and behaviours in these groups, speciesism is less likely to be called out.

If someone does call it out, they are often ignored or silenced. I have started to find some vegan spaces that promote *total liberation* where voices of those from marginalized groups are more prominent. In these spaces people understand or are willing to learn about systemic oppressions, where the connections between human and nonhuman oppressions are seen as important, and where it is understood that we need to include both humans and other animals in our anti-oppression stances. These are the spaces that need to become more representative of the vegan movement. (2017, p. 149)

That is not to say vegans should therefore abandon the fundamentals of intersectionality. Sebastian (2017a) himself is very clear that he "strongly and enthusiastically" supports the fundamentals of intersectional feminism and recognises their role within animal advocacy. The issue lies with the potentially misguided application and appropriation of a label that may not quite mesh with veganism in its original context. This may be the case by people who are themselves not of a marginalised or oppressed group but who are keen to be seen as acting as allies. Thus, they assume intersectionality as an identity rather than engaging with intersectionality as praxis. Praxis refers to the tying of critical thinking to critical acting to address oppression (Freire, 1970).

The exclusion from consideration of other marginalised communities from the scope of animal rights steers dangerously close towards eco-fascism. While the adoption of intersectional veganism as an identity may not prove to be an appropriate framework, where does this leave animal advocates? There have been many suggestions over the years, all consistent in their fundamentals. Sebastian (2017b) has suggested radical veganism as a concept that is the logical extension of a commitment to advocating for the rights of other animals to also include human communities. Radical vegans build communities and create solutions whilst actively demonstrating their commitment to anti-oppression. This involves the elevation of marginalised voices whilst simultaneously centring other animals within their own movement (Sebastian, 2017b). Best (2014) proposes the concept of total liberation that is essentially an anti-capitalist position with a critical understanding of the interrelation between all oppressions that recognises human, other animal and Earth liberation as inseparable. In 2018 Adams, Repka, Bailey and Brueck launched the *Bill of Consistent Anti-Oppression*, which Adams described at the 2018 VegFest UK as part of their work to bring veganism back to its roots (Adams, 2018). What are those roots? As Yates (2017) has stated, veganism has a focus, the human/other animal relationship. The founders of the vegan movement itself (as we know it) defined the scope of a more expansive ideal than is often realised. The Vegan Society expanded the definition as follows:

> A philosophy and way of living which seeks to exclude — as far as is possible and practicable — all forms of exploitation of, and cruelty to, animals for food, clothing or any other purpose; and by extension,

promotes the development and use of animal-free
alternatives for the benefit of animals, humans and
the environment. (1988, n.p.)

From the outset (and developed throughout its evolution) veganism and the pursuit of animal liberation has been
rooted in an understanding of social justice that was inclusive of humans within its scope. As Rodríguez states "no
social justice movement can truly succeed until it acknowl-
edges that it is just one piece of a larger Movement for a Just
Society" (2017, p. 29).

The inclusion of human rights within the scope of the
animal rights movement in no way detracts from the focus.
Rather, creating connections and understandings with other
individuals and communities (who are striving against the
same systems, states and corporations) can, in turn, create
a unified movement with a variety of foci, combining abil-
ities, resources and the sheer force of numbers required to
actualise justice for other animals and humans in a system-
ically unjust world. There is a reason why the intersections
of oppression so closely resemble the intersections of the
webs that constitute industrial complexes. One cannot be
dismantled without deconstructing the other. Further, that
may mean seeking connections in the unlikeliest of places.

It is often asked who could work in a slaughterhouse?
Rarely is it asked what sort of a society demands individuals
fulfil that role in the first place. Trauma relating to slaughterhouse work is widely documented, as are the commensurate

negative impacts upon the broader community. A 2016 study of South African slaughterhouse workers found that the "risk potential for employees suffering from post-traumatic stress syndrome was evident throughout the stages of being a slaughter-floor employee" (Victa & Bernard, 2016, p. 1). The study noted that employees are high-risk for adverse health effects including mental health and some of the "highest rates of injury in the manufacturing industry" (Victa & Bernard, 2016, p. 1). Slaughterhouse workers go through a process of desensitisation following their entry into the industry:

> My first time when I killed it was not easy for me. I feel pity for it. I felt I just wanted to close my eyes, turn around and run away. It was really sad but the more you do it the easier it gets. Like yesterday I had to shoot cows in the kraal [corral]. I climbed over the fence, walked over to the cow, and just shot it. I feel nothing any more. (Victa & Bernard, 2016, p. 1)

Another participant in their study described how his work killing cattle also resulted in violence towards the family companion animal "I can kick it if I want to because I kill cattle every day" (Victa & Bernard, 2016, p. 3). Feelings of empathy, compassion and guilt must be suppressed on the kill-floor and within the spaces either side. This emotional suppression can have significant impacts on the broader community. Richard, Signal & Taylor stated in their study into Queensland farmers and meatworkers, there is evidence "that there may be higher incidences of familial violence as well as other crimes and social problems among populations of meatworkers" (2013, p. 399). The increasing casualisation of the workforce (again as a result of neoliberal economic policy) has been "linked to the increased use of migrant workers who are more exploitable and self-exploiting than domestic workers which reduces the opportunity for collectivism" (McCabe & Hamilton, 2015, p. 96).

The relationship between animal advocates and workers in slaughter industries is typified by hostility, sometimes resulting in physical harm. In June 2020 the vegan and animal rights community was shocked by the killing of activist Regan Russel by a truck driver bearing pigs to slaughter at Fearman's Pork, Toronto (Rosella, 2020). Some people (most notably those with direct connections to the pig and trucking industries) chose to meet her death with further violence, both verbal and physical (Rankin, 2020). However, very occasionally advocates may have positive interactions with individuals employed by these industries, interactions that provide not only invaluable connections but profound insights into the psychology of the workers. I myself have had three memorable interactions, which I would like to share with you here:

- In 2018 Tasmanian Animal Save (now defunct) held their first vigil outside Tasmanian Quality Meats. We successfully stopped trucks bearing sheep to slaughter for most of the day, with some verbal abuse from workers wearing blood-stained protective clothing. Later in the day, a truck carrying tallow for rendering exited the facility, and the driver asked us if anyone required a lift or needed water. I engaged him in conversation, and he told me that he hated the "evil things that are done here" but that he had no alternative job opportunities, living as he was in a small rural area with a family and a limited education.

- At another facility one year later, a kill floor worker left the premises to stop for lunch at his house (which was situated next door to the slaughterhouse), still wearing his work-bloodied clothing. He was a migrant worker who was settled in the area under a regional migrant development scheme. He conveyed to us how much he disliked his job but that his access to alternatives was otherwise non-existent.

- In 2018, I participated in a peaceful occupation of the Luv-a-Duck slaughterhouse in Nhill. After five hours of documenting the facility and obstructing operations, we facilitated the liberation of 19 ducks from the kill line. Having run a duck off the premises (who I passed onto another quicker activist to swiftly transport to the awaiting vehicles) I was approached by a worker who at first said that what we were doing was wrong, that it was theft. During the course of the conversation he revealed that due to the nature of his work he could not consume the flesh of ducks, knowing how it was produced. Once again the question of job opportunities arose as an explanation for his remaining at the facility. Regional jobs outside of animal exploitation and slaughter are few and far

between. Our conversation ended with a hand shake
and he patted me on the back telling me to keep up
the good work.

I do not share these interactions to promote myself as
someone whose powers of communication are so advanced
that I am able to successfully 'vegan outreach' those people who are employed in slaughterhouses. This book is not
a click bait YouTube video. Rather, these are examples of
moments in time where even those with the most diamet-
rically opposed views can find common ground and share
our lived experiences. Job opportunities, the need to support
families, government immigration and employment policies
are recurrent themes in these and other interactions I have
had with individuals within the other animal flesh sector.
Private businesses and corporations exploit these people
as a means to obtain and maintain labour resources, to the
detriment of the individuals and to their surrounding communities. It is easy to demonise the worker who holds the
knife because their actions, who when caught on camera
are the most graphic expression of the violence inherent
within the system.

What if instead, the responsibility for that violence is laid
at the feet of a socio-political system that allows corporate
interests to engage in worker and community exploitation?
The elites of this system force individuals into institution-
alised violence against other animals, causing physical and
psychological suffering to both other animals and humans.
Consideration within the scope of veganism for migrant

workers and communities impacted by increased rates of violence associated with the meat industry could provide important in-roads into the industry itself. The lobbying for reskilling programs for workers seeking to exit the industry, and the relaxing of immigration restrictions that often tie migrant workers to jobs in regional areas with few other job opportunities could prove advantageous to dismantling the slaughter system. But efficacy of the lobbying would be dependent upon the interpersonal relationships fostered between those who stand on either side of the slaughterhouse gate. It is not a matter of putting the rights of other animals second to the rights of humans. It is about the strategic deconstruction of a vast system, thread by thread, until that web-like network can no longer support itself or be supported.

The inclusion of worker exploitation by the slaughter industries within the scope of animal liberation is often resisted by many within the vegan movement. Additionally, environmentalism is viewed by some in the vegan and animal rights communities as being a fringe or secondary concern to the promotion of the rights of other animals as sentient individuals. It has even been said that environmental concerns dilute the animal rights message or act as a distraction. This narrowed, single-issue perspective sadly overlooks a significant crossover between the environmental and animal rights spheres, and ignores the plight of other animals existing in the wild whose very lives are impacted by human industry. Once again, connections can be made through engaging environmentalists and creating a sharing of skills and resources which can only work to strengthen both movements. At one environmental protest action earlier in the year a forest defender said to me with obvious relief "thank fuck, the animal libbers are finally here."

In February 2020 I joined activists operating in takayna (otherwise known as the Tarkine Forest) working under The Bob Brown Foundation to protect an area of old-growth rainforest from logging approved and indeed financially supported by the Tasmanian state government via debt guarantees (Bolger, 2015). It was my first time entering a clear-fell coup and it was just like walking into a slaughterhouse. All around us were the strategically stacked bodies of felled eucalyptus obliqua, blackheart sassafras and nothofagus myrtle. Some of the trees were giants who were hundreds of years old, cut down to create specialist veneers for high-class hotels and homes, or for the woodchip export market. The ground was two metres deep with debris from the destroyed rainforest mid-canopy including dicksonia antarctica tree-ferns which can live for centuries if left undisturbed. During autumn, this debris is strategically napalmed to clear the land in preparation for the fast-growing cultivars of eucalyptus preferred by the logging industry. As we walked the coup to familiarise ourselves with the landscape, we saw signs of the other animals who once lived there. Clumps of possum fur and fledgling bird feathers were scattered around from the bodies of those who fled the chaos or could not flee the carnage in time. In some places you could smell the unmistakable stench of rotting flesh underfoot. Throughout the surrounding rainforest we saw evidence of burrowing crayfish who were crushed and killed by the machinery and felled trees. During the time of our stay a family of black cockatoos would circle periodically overhead, seemingly confused as they cried their mournful calls. The devastation wrought on those forests and their inhabitants by government and corporate greed was deeply confronting.

Following that occupation I assisted with two other actions in forests, one in the Wentworth Hills and one south of Hobart on Brown Mountain. Each time I have entered a clearfell that same feeling that we are standing in a slaughterhouse returns. Each time the relevance of forest protection to animal liberation is reinforced. The burrowing crayfish crushed by the bulldozer is no less worthy of our consideration and advocacy as the day old chick shredded in the macerator. The possum killed in the falling tree was as inherently deserving of life as the sow confined to a stall. The black cockatoo bereft of her nest is no less mournful than the dairy cow deprived of her calf. My experiences defending the forests of Tasmania have been shaped by my veganism and they are now inseparable. As Håkansson states:

> Deforestation for example, can be and is an environmental, human, Indigenous and animal rights issue. Veganism which considers all these elements can alleviate a wide range of negative impacts and sufferings. (2020, n.p.)

Indeed, the logging industry represents yet another

industrial complex with corporations creating cheap and specialty timber products. These products are for predominantly overseas markets utilising money poured into industry representative groups from the taxpayer purse. Fighting for the liberation of the forests from corporate and government greed is essential in the fight for total animal liberation as well as human and Earth liberation. Indeed, one might call it an urgent moral imperative.

However, to acknowledge the relevance of environmentalism to the message of animal liberation would necessitate some animal advocates to consider the ethics of their own behaviours, even though they may be already vegan. There is a moral need to question what is consumed and how, the ways people travel or build homes, the corporations that society is willing to financially support and the ways each individual moves through and lives in this world. Just as the average non-vegan may be resistant to the concept of veganism, so too are many vegans resistant to the idea that maybe veganism is not as inherently honourable as was once thought and that maybe there are further changes vegans all must make to be truly consistent. It is this resistance that even vegans demonstrate towards making individual consumer changes that large corporations rely upon in order to maintain market availability even when the consumer demographic shifts.

The market proliferation of plant-based products has increased significantly in the past five years. In Australia Hungry Jacks, Dominos, Pizza Hut, Coles and Woolworths have released plant-based ranges proudly emblazoned with the vegan label. Overseas KFC, Burger King, Taco Bell and Denny's all now include vegan options on their menus. Beyond Meats and the controversial Impossible Burger have dominated fast food markets, attracting floods of plant-based eaters to food outlets they otherwise would have avoided. As a business model, this tactic has largely paid off for business owners. The release of the Impossible Whopper by Burger King in 2019 resulted in a boost in sales and an increase of sales in the traditional cow flesh Whopper (Taylor, 2019). As it stands the Impossible burger itself is not a vegan product, with lethal testing on rats commissioned by Impossible Foods to secure approval from the US Food and Drug Administration (FDA), despite this approval not being necessary for the sale of the product (Newkey-Burden, 2019). Around the same time, Tyson Foods announced they were launching a new range of pea-protein 'chicken', an announcement that was lauded by some populist vegans as a sign that veganism was winning. Tyson Foods kills 2 billion individual chickens per year and shows no signs of reducing that number despite this revolutionary new product line (Durbin, 2019). Back in Australia, despite the increased plant-based ranges available on supermarket shelves, meat sales are not decreasing. Between them, Woolworths and Coles have captured over 50% of the $13 billion Australian meat market, all whilst increasing plant-based options on their shelves, including many under their own brands (Roy Morgan, 2018). The volume of the slaughter is staggering, with a projected 660 million chickens alone to be slaughtered in the year 2020 (Australian Bureau of Statistics, 2020).

What is being witnessed here are manifestations of successful green-washing and humane-washing campaigns created by corporations that are responsible for widespread harm to other animals, humans and the environment. These campaigns capitalise on imagery, language and even colour-schemes to promote environmentalism or a humane positioning that is simply not based in reality. According to Nixon, these transnational corporations are "potent, active players in manufacturing the icons and stories that shape popular perceptions of environmental science and policy" (2011, p. 38). The vast majority of the public are buying it. The release of a plant-based Milo by Nestle earlier in 2020 was met by widespread excitement amongst the vegan community. This is despite Nestle's ongoing history of child trafficking for cocoa production, their role in rainforest degradation contributing to species diversity loss and their siphoning of water resources via government approved permits to sell as bottled water (Gilbreath, 2017). The former Nestle chief executive and chairman stated in 2005 that water was a "grocery product" and not inherently a human right (Gilbreath, 2017). In 2020 Lindt announced work on a line of vegan chocolate products, again lauded by populist mainstream vegan leaders. The company is unable to guarantee a cocoa supply chain free from child trafficking and continues to exploit cows for the creation of their other chocolate products (Peyton, 2019). Critical consideration needs to be given to the impacts these corporations have on humans and on the natural world. Additionally, consideration needs to be given to how profits are typically utilised for research and development to maximise the efficiency of product creation as well as market expansion. It is not then possible to view the creation of plant-based products as remotely indicative that the realisation of animal liberation is closer to hand.

Naive protestations of supply and demand overlook the role of the state in funding corporations, expanding markets and subsidising individual producers and businesses. These strategies also overlook government interference in foreign markets to create systems of debt through trade-based colonisation. Consider the US stockpile of 'government cheese' where in 2016 the US Department of Agriculture (USDA) utilised taxpayer monies to purchase 5000 tonnes of cheese as a means to reduce the cheese surplus and stabilise milk price fluctuations (Yates, 2016). This policy recalls the mass subsidies granted to grain producers under Roosevelt that resulted in the birth of the CAFO discussed in the first essay. The cheese is utilised by the USDA in its Commodity Supplemental Food Program as part of a strategy to feed elderly people who fit the requirements for food assistance (USDA, 2020). Oversupply of cheese resulted in a surplus that necessitated government intervention to address, utilising the poverty of the community to create viable market conditions. The demand was not there, it was artificially manufactured.

No amount of people 'going vegan' can prevent government intervention in the market facilitation of its own wealth creation interests. At best, the corresponding proliferation of plant-based products may potentially innovate some facets of human food systems. At worst (the most realistic outcome) the proliferation is a deliberate corporate ploy that utilises the pairing of quick consumer culture with the increasing absorption of human attention by social media platforms. According to Nixon "the plasticity of brain circuits are reprogrammed by a digital world that threatens to 'info-whelm' us into a state of perpetual distraction" (2011, p. 12). The public and vegans in particular, are not being provided with plant-based options rather they are being strategically distracted. And what are they being distracted from? The pursuit of justice, as the public's attention becomes consumed by consumption and the vegan movement becomes further ensnared within the corporate web.

Thus far, it appears that the most significant achievement of apolitical vegan consumerism has been the commensurate increase in corporate profit margins. What has largely been perceived as liberation in a burger wrapper has not reduced the numbers of other animals on the kill line. The numbers of other animals slaughtered for human consumption continues to climb; rainforests continue to be destroyed; non-domesticated animals continue to be killed and displaced; humans are pushed further into poverty and subjected to increasing rates of pollution, worker exploitation and trafficking continues; Indigenous communities are dispossessed and brutalised; activists for other animal, human and Earth rights continue to be murdered (see, for example, Global Witness reports in Harrison, 2017). The liberation of other animals from human exploitation cannot be facilitated without simultaneously addressing those systems of exploitation and oppression that also affect humans and the environment. It is imperative that vegans create connections with other social justice movements and include them within the scope of the vegan movement. But more than that, vegans must begin the work necessary to connect to individuals and communities who exist within the very industries that need dismantling. The activist task is to manifest programs that could result in their liberation from the kill floor as well as releasing other animals from the kill line. An understanding of focus and scope, and the global issue of interconnectivity is paramount to pulling the threads of the animal industrial complex and related webs.

References

Adams, C. (2018). *Transcript: London VegFest 2018.* https://www. consistentantioppression. com/transcriptlondonvegfest2018

Amnesty International (2020). *Lion: Help stop human rights abuses in Myanmar.* https://action. amnesty.org.au/act-now/ demand-kirin-divest-from-myanmar-military

Anarchists Worldwide (2020). *Goodbye Walter Bond.* https:// anarchistsworldwide.noblogs.org/post/2020/07/27/ua-goodbye-walterbond/

Animal Charity Evaluators (2018). *Trends in meat production.* https://animalcharityevaluators.org/research/other-topics/ trends-in-meat-production/

Australian Bureau of Statistics (ABS) (2020). *Livestock products.* https://www.abs.gov.au/statistics/industry/agriculture/ livestock-products-australia/latest-release

Batt, E. (1964). *Why veganism?* https://www.abolitionistapproach. com/text/why-veganism-by-eva-batt/

Best, S. (2014). *The politics of total liberation: Revolution for the 21st century.* Palgrave MacMillan.

Bloch, H., & Ferguson, F. (Eds.). (1989/2020). *Misogyny, misandry and misanthropy.* University of California.

Bolger, R. (2015). *Forestry Tasmania debt guarantee increased to $41 million by state government.* https://www.abc.net.au/

news/2015-06-09/forestry-tasmania-debt-guarantee-quadrupled-to-41-million/6531816

Braidotti, R. (2013). *The posthuman*. Polity.

Brueck, J. (2017). *Veganism in an oppressive world: A vegans of color community project*. Sanctuary Publishers.

Centers for Disease Control and Prevention (2017). *Zoonotic diseases*. https://www.cdc.gov/onehealth/basics/zoonotic-diseases.html

Centers for Disease Control Prevention (2019). *Antibiotic resistance threats in the United States 2019*. https://www.cdc.gov/drugresistance/pdf/threats-report/2019-ar-threats-report-508.pdf

Crenshaw, K. (1989). Demarginalizing the intersection of race and sex: A black feminist critique of antidiscrimination doctrine, feminist theory and antiracist politics. *University of Chicago Legal Forum, 1989*(1), 139-167.

Cross, L. (1954). The surge of freedom. *The Vegan, 9*(3), 9-12.

Doherty, P., & Shields, M. (2017). *Piggery plans hit the wall but controversy continues over who has the right to farm in south-west NSW*. https://www.abc.net.au/news/rural/2017-02-03/harden-piggery-plans-hit-wall/8239464

Donaldson, S., & Kymlicka, W. (2011). *Zoopolis: A political theory of animal rights*. Oxford University Press.

Durbin, D. (2019). *Tyson is the latest player to enter hot plant-based meat market.* https://fortune.com/2019/06/13/tyson-plant-based-meat-pea-protein

Foer, J., & Gross, A. (2020). *We have to wake up: Factory farms are breeding grounds for pandemics.* https://www.theguardian.com/commentisfree/2020/apr/20/factory-farms-pandemic-risk-covid-animal-human-health

Francione, G. (2016). *Veganism as a moral imperative.* https://www.abolitionistapproach.com/veganism-moral-imperative/

Freire, P. (1970). *Pedagogy of the oppressed.* Continuum International Publishing.

Gilbreath, A. (2017). *Nestlé is sucking the world's aquifers dry.* https://longreads.com/2017/10/04/nestle-is-sucking-the-worlds-aquifers-dry

Håkansson, E. (2020). *Is veganism only about animals?* https://www.farmtransparency.org/editorials/231-is-veganism-only-about-animals

Haraway, D. (2008). *When species meet.* Minnesota, USA: University of Minnesota.

Harrison, A. (2017). *Worst year ever for environmental and land rights activists.* www.globalwitness.org/en/press-releases/worst-year-ever-environmental-and-land-rights-activists-least-200-killed-2016-crisis-spreads-across-globe/

Helmore, E. (2020). *Activists sour on Oatly vegan milk after stake sold to Trump-linked Blackstone*. https://www.theguardian.com/food/2020/sep/01/oatly-vegan-milk-sale-blackstone

Kassam, L. (2017). Interview. In J. Brueck (Ed.), *Veganism in an oppressive world: A vegans of color community project* (pp. 148-49). Sanctuary Publishers.

Ko, S. (2016). We can avoid the debate about comparing human and animal oppressions, if we simply make the right connections. In A. Ko & S. Ko (Eds.), *Aphro-ism: Essays on pop culture, feminism, and Black veganism from two sisters* (pp. 82-87). Lantern Books.

Lymery, P., & Oakeshott, I. (2014). *Farmageddon: The true cost of cheap meat*. Bloomsbury.

Manavis, S. (2018). *Eco-fascism: The ideology marrying environmentalism and white supremacy thriving online*. https://www.newstatesman.com/science-tech/social-media/2018/09/eco-fascism-ideology-marrying-environmentallism-and-white-supremacy

Mason, J. (2005). *An unnatural order: Why we are destroying the planet and each other*. Lantern Books.

Mason, M., & McDowell, R. (2020). *Investigation finds widespread labor abuses in palm oil industry*. https://agrinews-pubs.com/2020/11/19/investigation-finds-widespread-labor-abuses-in-palm-oil-industry/afuj2d4/

McCabe, D., & Hamilton, L. (2015). The kill programme: an ethnographic study of 'dirty work' in a slaughterhouse. *New Technology, Work and Employment, 30*(2), 95-108.

National Geographic (2020). *Jainism.* https://www. nationalgeographic.org/encyclopedia/jainism/

Newkey-Burden, C. (2019). *Sorry vegans, Burger King's impossible whopper won't do anything to save animals.* https://www. independent.co.uk/burger-king-vegan-impossible-whopper-animal-testing-peta-a8854481.html

Nixon, R. (2011). *Slow violence and the environmentalism of the poor.* Harvard University Press.

NonZeroSum (2020). *The bizarre case of vegan neo-nazis and why we need to work on deprogramming vegans who glorify violence.* https://philosophicalvegan.com/viewtopic.php?f=7&t=7202

Oguh, C. (2020). *Blackstone's Schwarzman emerges as Wall Street's top political donor.* https://www.reuters.com/article/us-usa-election-blackstone-schwarzman-idUSKBN2601NA

Opotow, S. (2018). Social justice theory and practice: Fostering inclusion in exclusionary contexts. In P. Hammack Jnr. (Ed.), *The Oxford book of social psychology and social justice* (pp. 41-56). Oxford University Press.

Peyton, N. (2019). *Made with child labor? Major chocolate companies flunk scorecard.* https://uk.reuters.com/article/us-usa-cocoa-childlabor/made-with-child-labor-major-chocolate-companies-flunk-scorecard-idUSKBN1WP34L

Rankin, C. (2020). *Animal rights advocates, counter-protesters clash at slaughterhouse where activist died.* https://www.cbc.ca/news/canada/hamilton/regan-russell-animal-rights-activists-protesters-1.5668891

Richard, E., Signal, T., & Taylor, N. (2013). A different cut? Comparing attitudes toward animals and propensity for aggression within two primary cohorts — farmers and meatworkers. *Society and Animals, 21*(4), 395-413.

Rodriguéz, S. (2017). Intersectionality versus diversity: A note to vegan organisations. In J. Brueck (Ed.), *Veganism in an oppressive world: A vegans of color community project* (pp. 24-31). Sanctuary Publishers.

Rosella, L. (2020). *Truck driver charged in incident at Burlington slaughterhouse that left animal rights protester dead.* https://www.thestar.com/news/gta/2020/07/20/truck-driver-charged-in-incident-at-burlington-slaughterhouse-that-left-animal-rights-protester-dead.html

Roy Morgan (2018). *It's official: Majority of fresh meat now bought at Coles & Woolworths.* https://www.roymorgan.com/findings/7562-supermarket-currency-report-fresh-meat-december-2017-201804130556

Ryder, R. (2010). Speciesism again: The original leaflet. *Critical Society,* Iss. 2, 1-2.

Sebastian, C. (2017a). *Yes to intersectionality, boo to intersectional veganism.* https://strivingwithsystems.com/2017/05/10/yes-to-intersectionality-boo-to-intersectional-vegans

Sebastian, C. (2017b). *Exploring radical veganism.* https://strivingwithsystems.com/2017/05/15/exploring-radical-veganism

Standaert, M. (2020). *'Mixed with prejudice': Calls for ban on 'wet' markets misguided, experts argue.* https://www.theguardian.com/environment/2020/apr/15/mixed-with-prejudice-calls-for-ban-on-wet-markets-misguided-experts-argue-coronavirus

Taylor, B., & Zimmerman, M. (2008). Deep ecology. In B. Taylor (Ed.), *Encyclopaedia of religion and nature* Vol. 1 (531-32). Bloomsbury.

Taylor, A. (2013). *Reconfiguring the natures of childhood.* Routledge.

Taylor, K. (2019). *Burger King's bet on faux meat is paying off as the impossible whopper convinces customers to spend more and buy more beef whoppers.* https://markets.businessinsider.com/news/stocks/impossible-whopper-boosts-burger-king-sales-2019-9-1028489082

The Vegan Society (2020). *Definition of veganism.* https://vegansociety.com/go-vegan/definition-veganism

Twine, R. (2012). Revealing the 'animal-industrial complex': A concept and method for critical animal studies. *Journal for Critical Animal Studies*, 10(1), 12-39.

Unilever (2020). *Unilever sets bold new 'Future Foods' ambition.* https://www.unilever.com/news/press-releases/2020/unilever-sets-bold-new-future-foods-ambition-html

United States Department of Agriculture (USDA). (2020). *Commodity supplemental food program.* https://www.fns.usda.gov/csfp/commodity-supplemental-food-program

Victa, K., & Bernard, A. (2016). Slaughtering for a living: A hermeneutic phenomenological perspective on the well-being of slaughterhouse employees. *The International Qualitative Studies on Health & Well-being, 11*(1) 1-13.

Watson, D. (1944). *The vegan news: Quarterly magazine of the non-dairy vegetarians.* https://issuu.com/vegan_society/docs/the_vegan_news_1944

Watts, J. (2015). *Gender, health and healthcare.* Ashgate.

Yates, J. (2016). *US to buy cheese to help milk prices and feed the poor.* https://www.fwi.co.uk/business/markets-and-trends/dairy-markets/us-buy-cheese-help-milk-prices-feed-poor

Yates, R. (2017). *Veganism's defining issues: Focus & scope.* https://onhumanrelationswithother sentientbeings.weebly.com/veganisms-defining-issues-focus-scope

Animal liberation and the carceral state

Foucault once asked whether it was surprising that prisons resemble many other institutions in society such as schools, army barracks and factories (1977, p. 233). Certainly the rigid conformity of those physical spaces bears the comparison. However, this was not a simple comparison between the physical spaces of those institutions. Rather, Foucault was viewing the school, the barracks and the factory as fulfilling a similar mechanism of control as the prison, as a space within which individuals become entirely reliant upon those in a position of authority. The authority figures control how the individual is required to behave, their productivity and how they will be treated within that space. In contemporary society this treatment is often based upon the perceived marginal status of the individual which can be influenced by the divisions of race, Indigeneity, disability, sexuality, gender or class (Thompson, 2018). Therefore, I argue Australian society is a carceral society as the systems and institutions that create and support the existence of prisons as a means of punishment and control inform and interact with other systems and social institutions, including the animal industrial complex. In this essay I will explore the many ways in which the carceral state and the systems that facilitate the exploitation and execution of other animals intersect. I argue the human relationship with other animals is fundamentally carceral in nature.

Foucault's comparison between the prison and these social institutions is applicable to the authoritarian spaces of facilities within the modern intensive farming system. In both physical structure and ideological intent the similarities between the human prison and the industrialised other animal exploitation facility are manifestly observable. The impacts extend throughout the other animal communities incarcerated within and beyond, to the human communities who work there or live in close proximity. It would be easy to draw an analogy between the workers in animal facilities and the guards in human prisons. Yet a recognition of the exploitation of those workers by management and corporate interests can yield a more profound understanding of how power is exercised and reinforced in the animal industrial complex. The physical and spatial similarities are somewhat obvious. Tall fences ringed with barbed wire, gates fastened with chains and locks and individuals confined within singular or group accommodation (cages) according to their status or ascribed function are observable in both the human prison and other animal prisons, such as pig farms or vivisection laboratories. The deprivation of both liberty and of contact with one's own kind as a form of punishment or experiment is a common occurrence. For example, the use of solitary confinement as a punitive measure for humans, or as part of maternal deprivation studies in primates.

Singer (2002) spends some time in *Animal liberation* describing the horrors of maternal deprivation studies involving primates. He states "many experiments inflict severe pain without the remotest prospect of significant benefits for human beings or any other animals. Such experiments are not isolated instances, but part of a major industry" (Singer, 2009, p. 36). The use of solitary confinement as a disciplinary tool within human prisons has reportedly led to an increase in mental health problems, including depression, anxiety and aggression (Weir, 2012). One must question what benefit this is to the individual prisoner who will likely find themselves released or to the communities into which they are released. Additionally, the isolating methods of transport used to transfer the human and the other animal prisoner also bear similarities. The enclosed compartmentalised vehicles offer the bare minimum space and safety (and often low standards of hygiene, as I have personally witnessed inside a police 'paddy wagon') necessary for the delivery of the individual to the courthouse or the slaughterhouse for 'processing.'

Some would argue that here is where the similarities end, both physically and ideologically, due to the perceived innocence of other animals. They commit no crimes deserving of incarceration and slaughter. Others may believe that human prisons as a punitive system perform a vital role in maintaining the order of society and should continue to do so. This practice is part of a social order that is dictated by legislators and enforced by their employees, the police and prison wardens. But this is a superficial understanding of how these systems operate in concert with one another as part of the prison and animal industrial complexes. The prison is an inherently political tool that is used to suppress dissent, to contain perceived social deviance and to effectively warehouse individuals deemed to have no place in society. As Davis states "the prison has become a black hole into which the detritus of contemporary capitalist society is deposited" (2003, p. 16). Many individuals find themselves incarcerated not because they inherently deserve to be placed in a cage. Rather, it is because of a series of political, ideological or socio-economic circumstances that render them unviable participants within the modern input/consumption-output/production system that provides the foundations of a capitalist society. A 2014 study of pre-incarceration incomes of people imprisoned in the US showed that incarcerated people had a median income that was 41% less than non-incarcerated people of a similar age, fractionally above the poverty line (Rauby & Kopf, 2015).

In the act of human incarceration, the neoliberal state creates an environment in which imprisoned bodies can be made profitable. This can involve privately owned prisons via the contracts to provide staff and resources, or through the exploitation of the imprisoned labour force itself. In

California, inmates were trained and employed to fight dangerous wild fires for low to no wages and potentially shortened sentences, but were until recently barred from employment as fire-fighters on release due to being felons (Hartman, 2020). In September 2020 the law AB 2147 was introduced that would expunge the records of people convicted of low level felonies who worked as fire fighters while incarcerated, thus enabling them to become employed in that sector upon release (Hartman, 2020). Australian prisons also make extensive use of their incarcerated labour force. Workers are paid as little as 82c per hour to manufacture a wide range of products from household goods to headsets for Qantas airlines, working in salt mines and even manufacturing the national flag (Brook, 2017). Prisoners receive no superannuation and their employers are not required to pay payroll tax. Thus, the neoliberal state has made the warehouses of the detritus of capitalist society into a viable resource and labour market.

Other animals are likewise considered nonviable participants in the capitalist system unless their lives and bodies are incarcerated and exploited for human gain as units of productivity. Humans have effectively criminalised animality itself. According to Wyckoff:

> Animality involves intersecting features of animals' lives, features which are constructed according to the ways in which particular animals or classes of animals are situated within human institutions and practices. (2015, p. 545)

That is to say, the species traits of individuals and of communities of other animals and how those traits can be utilised, restrained or exterminated by humans is what defines animality. This anthropocentric ideology effectively criminalises other animals by right of them not being human. This criminalisation has occurred to the extent that other animals are punished for their perceived transgressions against humans in often public demonstrations of violence against the transgressors. Others are subsumed within the confines of human society and altered both physically and psychologically according to social demands. No matter how innocent other animals may be, they are made deserving of carceral control and violence by simply being animals in a human dominated world.

The othering of human prisoners refers to the physical and ideological separation of marginalised individuals from mainstream society (Seidman, 2016). Othering is used as a means to justify not only their incarceration but also the exploitation of their labour. This view has become normalised to the extent that the broader community struggles to recognise the inherent function of the prison system as a mechanism for control, instead viewing it as normal, natural and necessary to the exclusion of all alternatives. This same argument is applied to our continued exploitation of other animals based upon a perceived 'natural' order. Sentient beings are strategically othered as a mechanism designed to turn individuals into machine-like entities, the primary function of which is as a unit of production. This dysfunctional relationship is described by Wadiwel as a strategic aggression against other animals, in which "property and commodification cohabit as artefacts of war" (2015, p. 147). Just as the state exerts property rights over the imprisoned human whilst commodifying their very incarceration, so too are other animals made the property of state-sponsored industry. The productivity (and reproductivity) of their bodies are subsequently commodified within the confines of their cage. The physical location of that cage is likewise important to guarantee its functionality to remove the incarcerated individual (human or other animal) from society. Further, and perhaps more importantly the aim is to "remove from sight, and responsibility, the violence that is inherent to its functioning" (Wadiwel, 2015, p. 195). The walls, locks and cages, and the separation from affluent urbanised areas that are observable in both the human and other animal prison systems are not merely physical similarities. They are strategically designed and deliberately applied to obscure the violence and deprivations inflicted upon those held inside the facilities from the view of the community. This process of obscuring assists in the absolution of the community of their responsibility for those incarcerated within.

There are of course differences manifest between human and other animal prison systems. For one, the majority of human prisoners will eventually leave the physical cage alive, notwithstanding deaths in custody and those held on death row. However, the processes of institutionalisation and continued social exclusion represent a psychological and sometimes physical cage that many former imprisoned persons will struggle to be free from. As Haney states:

> Thus, institutionalization or prisonization renders some people so dependent upon external constraints that they gradually lose the capacity to rely on internal organization and self-imposed personal limits to hide their actions and restrain their conduct. If and when this external structure is taken away, severely institutionalized persons may find that they no longer know how to do things on their own, or how to refrain from doing those things that are ultimately harmful or self-destructive. (2001, n.p.)

These same behaviours have been observed in dogs who have either been bred in or rescued from puppy farms. Institutionalisation in these facilities can lead to dogs exhibiting fear and aggression, anxiety and an array of other emotional and physical problems that are often difficult to rehabilitate (McMillan, 2017). Adapting to life outside of a cage can be challenging for human and non-human alike.

This is not to draw a direct analogy between human and other animal prisoners, especially given the disproportionate infliction of police brutality and incarceration enforced by the state against Black, Indigenous and People of Colour (BIPOC) communities. There is an extensive history of white supremacy being enforced through the "animalisation" of Black and Indigenous peoples as a justification for exploitation and oppression that needs to be acknowledged and addressed. As Ko explains:

For people who are routinely animalized and considered sub-human, we can have a different relationship
to animal oppression. It doesn't feel as external to us as
it might for a person who gets the advantage of being
considered 'human.' (cited in Vegan Life, 2017, n.p.)

Additionally, Best states that:

[...] the argument is not that human and animal
experiences and forms of oppression are identical or
that there are no salient differences to be drawn, but
rather that the similarities are more important than
the differences. (2014, p. 32)

I do not entirely agree with him. The differences are
equally as important as the similarities when dissecting the
oppressive systems. The ways in which differences are understood and acted upon can say a lot about who an individual
person truly is. As Ko states:

[…] by proving a meaningful continuity between
these groups or proving they are significantly alike
us in ways that are important to the privileged group,
we thereby lose reasons for differential allocation
of resources or protections, and so on, and effect a
change in treatment owed to the marginalized group
in question. (2015, p. 40)

When devalued differences are placed within the context
of the history of their usage to perpetuate the oppression of
humans it behoves humans to tread carefully and with respect.

The justice task is to compare and critique the systems and the impacts of those systems on individuals and communities without fetishising or further oppressing the victims.

As a tool utilised in the suppression of political dissent, the carceral system is fundamentally obstructive to the realisation of other animal liberation. This is achieved through the persecution and incarceration of those individuals who challenge the authority of the state and the law in the pursuit of justice. As discussed in the first essay, governments will expend considerable energy and resources in altering legal codes as a response to the growing activists' groups which challenge the animal industrial complex. To support the continuation of the prison state is to support a system that operates in direct opposition to the fundamental ideals of liberation itself. Animal advocates know that because a cause is just in their eyes does not render them immune from the law, however oppressive that law may be.

Other animals have long been held to account for their perceived crimes against humans, through the application of incarceration, the infliction of pain, and execution, even under the human justice system. Pliny the Elder (23-79 CE) wrote of the ceremonial retribution wrought against the dogs of Rome for their historical failure to warn the city of an attack by the Gauls:

> We have already spoken of the honours earned by the geese, when the Gauls were detected in their attempt to scale the Capitol. It is for a corresponding

reason, also, that punishment is yearly inflicted upon the dogs, by crucifying them alive upon a gibbet of elder, between the Temple of Juventas and that of Summanus. (Pliny, c. 77CE/1991)

The ceremony of the *supplicia canum* (which translates to 'the punishment of the dogs') made the punishment of dogs for the sins of their forebears a public spectacle. By tying the religious ceremony of torture to the protection of the state, the geese were rewarded for saving Rome and the dogs were destroyed. Whilst this may seem a particularly barbaric relic of the past, the public torture and execution of other animals has continued into the modern era. In 1916 an elephant named Mary was hanged in Erwin (East Tennessee) for the crime of killing her handler. Five hundred spectators attended the old rail depot, where Mary was hanged by the neck from a crane until dead (Schroeder, 2009). She was not the first elephant to be executed in the US. In 1903 Topsy was poisoned, strangled and eventually electrocuted in front of a crowd of invited guests and the press for the 'crime' of killing a circus spectator. Topsy developed 'behavioural problems' due to the abuse and mishandling she was subjected to by her owners and handlers (Daly, 2013). These executions are reminiscent of the public spectacles of hanging with Ronald Ryan being the last person hanged in Australia in 1967. However, the practice of public hangings had ceased by the end of the 1850s by which time they had come to be regarded as horrific spectacles belonging to the past.

The presence of the public at executions was originally an integral part of the ceremony itself. Foucault described the public in attendance as being "the main character" and he explains that:

> The aim was to make an example, not only by making people aware that the slightest offence was likely to be punished, but by arousing feelings of terror by the spectacle of power letting its anger fall upon the guilty person. (1977, p. 58)

Long after the execution was over the memory of the killing inflicted by the state remained in the individual and public psyche. In recognising the humanity of the person on the scaffold, no matter how heinous their crime, the member of the public would thus internalise the message 'there but for the grace of God go I.' It also follows that the public executions of other animals elicited some empathy for the hapless victim. Thus, over the years the sight of violence against other animals has been increasingly withdrawn from the public gaze. Similarly, the violence of the human carceral system has been obscured to increasing degrees with the construction of the modern prison. Today however, the accessibility of technology has enabled the public to record and disseminate footage of police brutality which is disproportionately enacted against BIPOC individuals and communities, and people living with mental illness or neurodivergence (Mapping Police Violence, 2020; Alexiou, 2020). Such footage has the power to spark global protest movements in pursuit of justice and change as the contemporary

Black Lives Matter movement and the uprisings following the killing of George Floyd by police has shown (Brara, 2020).

So too does the dissemination of footage of state enforced violence against other animals have a potentially transformative effect. Now when the punishment of other animals is exposed to the broader public, the response is typically one of horror. In 1994 Tyke the elephant killed one trainer and critically injured two other men. After escaping the circus that held her captive Tyke was shot 86 times by police, before collapsing and dying in the street. Her public execution was documented and widely broadcast leading to lawsuits against her owner and his company, against the City of Honolulu and the State of Hawaii (Hoover, 2004). Tyke's name was invoked when after almost 25 years Hawaii became the second state of the US to ban the importation and use of wild animals in circuses or carnivals (Hawaii State Legislature, 2018). The memory of her tortured face, immortalised by photographers who captured the torment of her final moments, pervades the public psyche to this day. However this transformative potential is largely limited to other animals outside of farming systems due to an ingrained speciesism. Though it can be assumed some individuals have chosen to eschew the consumption of animal products as a result of the dissemination of footage from within farming facilities.

As such, the use of investigations into such facilities as a tool to undermine systems of oppression should not be undervalued. It must be said, however, that there are some who are more profoundly affected by footage of the mistreatment of other animals than they are by footage of police executing Black people. More than a few vegans have gone so far as to seek to justify such acts even though racism should be regarded as oppositional to the fundamental ideals of veganism. How individuals react to such footage is entirely informed by their own prejudices, vegan or not.

This rejection of the public spectacle of animal executions was manifest in the outrage generated by a controversial piece of performance art hosted by the Dark MOFO festival in Tasmania in 2017. Austrian artist Hermann Nitsch (who is infamous for his works involving animal carcasses and blood) brought *150.Action* to Hobart a work that would necessitate the collection of blood from twelve slaughtered steers, the killing of multiple fishes, and the slaughter of specifically chosen one bull (upon whose killing the public outrage was fixated). Actors and dancers were employed to carry the crucified body of the slain bull into an arena, whereupon his flesh would be torn from his bones. The actors would then roll in the blood and flesh in what the artist himself describes as an act that "rummages around in the joy in cruelty; chaos, and orgiastic intoxication, irrupts and breaks in over us" (Nitsch, 2020). The piece united vegans with non-vegans, seasoned activists, sanctuary owners and politicians with everyday concerned citizens as a campaign to prevent and eventually disrupt the event dominated the public discourse. Despite a six-week long campaign that included media saturation and the deliberate disruption of ticketing by activists, the bull was executed and the event went ahead.

The identity of the individual bull was never revealed but he nevertheless became an icon, emblematic of the ongoing human persecution of other animals. Though his death was not itself performed publicly (rather, within the confines of a slaughterhouse situated away from the city centre somewhere in the south), the brutality meted out against this one bull in the pursuit of artistic endeavour threw the dysfunctionality of our relationships with other animals into stark relief, forcing us to confront a reality we prefer to shy away from. But unlike Tyke, Mary and Topsy, the Dark MOFO Bull was not accused of a perceived 'crime' against a human. His very animality was his crime and was used as justification for his execution. He was an animal, therefore the human could do to him what they chose, whether for the purpose of food or in the pursuit of artistic endeavour. In crossing the line of public spectacle, though, Nitsch raised the ire of a public desperate to cling to a wilful ignorance created by the construction of walls, gates and legislation that prevent us from acknowledging our role in the perpetration of violence against other animals, providing a salve to the guilty human conscience.

Humans are adept at ascribing criminality to other animals as a means to justify our meting out punishments upon them, even now in the 21st century (though the advance of years should not be regarded as an indicator of social progress). It is common practice across the Australian continent for graziers to trap and shoot wild dogs and dingos then nail their bodies to the limbs of trees. In an interview with the

ABC, one professional shooter called the animals cruel due to their alleged surplus killing of sheep and native animals, that is the killing of other animals without the need for food (Lloyd, 2017). This cruelty is used by many as a justification for the wholesale eradication of the animals whether wild dog or dingo (the distinction is important to conservationists, less so to proponents of animal rights). The display of their slain corpses is used as a means to communicate the numbers being killed, or as a political statement. Lloyd reports that:

> [...] a head stockman and manager in south-west and central Queensland, says the carcasses can also be a form of protest by graziers. In a post on Facebook group Ringers from the Top End, he said stringing dogs up started as a political statement to make people aware of the devastation they cause to livestock and livelihoods, and as a complaint against the lack of action taken by the Government. "That is why you see them hung on road signs or beside roads". (2017, n.p.)

The crime of the wild dog or the dingo is to engage in the natural expression of their animality. Their slain bodies are used as a political statement in a similar way to the human hanging from the gibbet. It is not just the wild dogs and dingoes who are subjected to this fate; cats, foxes, kangaroos, pigs, all are targeted for the crime of being animals in a world dominated by humans. They threaten the well-being of grazing farm animals whose bodies are likewise controlled and brutalised by humans (and, perhaps more importantly, the profits extracted from that brutality). All have their bodies placed on display to communicate that dominance. In 2019 I visited a sheep farm to collect a lamb who had been rejected by her mother. The farmer was most concerned for the individual welfare of the lamb but drew the line at the ravens whose slain bodies he had strung along his barbed wire fences as a warning to other ravens in the area. "Bloody things peck the eyes out of the ewes and get at the lambs, and I can't have that," he told me.

Though these are examples of the public display of punishments inflicted upon other animals, the communities to which that display is communicated are often limited in size. Regional areas are sparsely populated and visitors transient. So they remain largely unseen by the broader public except on those occasions where images of the victims of these punishments are shared via social media. At that time the relevant information can become muddied amidst the war of words that inevitably erupts. But there are areas of daily life within the urban space where the punishments meted out against other animals are apparent, if the public allow themselves to see them for what they are. As Wadiwel states:

> The urban spheres of the West represent a 'gulag archipelago' (or from Foucault, a 'carceral archipelago') of interlinked forms of containment, delegated authority, everyday violences and surveillances; a system of 'grand' apartheid supported by an equally precise system of everyday 'petty' apartheid. (2015, p. 200)

The streets through which humans move, the buildings humans inhabit, and the structural boundaries humans erect around and within their homes are designed to either keep out or contain other animals as humans so chose. Even the most seemingly benign relationships between humans and other animals, such as companionship, are predicated upon a series of behavioural and physical alterations to the individual animal to ensure their conformity within the boundaries of the human space. Unchecked animality cannot be permitted to exist within the domestic realm. Thus, humans erect fences, perform invasive medical procedures upon them such as de-sexing and require the companion animal to fit around their lifestyles and schedules, sometimes with limited reciprocation. That is not to say that the relationship between the family and the family dog is not one of emotional connection, nor that humans should entirely abandon the canine to their fate in the wild or on the streets. But it should be recognised that humans' relationship with companion animals is a relationship of control nevertheless, no matter how paternalistically benign.

Zoos and aquariums perhaps bear the most obvious similarity to the human prison. However they retain the spectacle of punishment in the form of control and loss of autonomy. This occurs through a range of enclosures and with an invitation open to the public to see each animal inmate in their individual confined area (for a price). Whereas the state will go to great lengths to ensure the human prison remains hidden from view. Millions of dollars will be poured into the construction of walls and security with the express purpose of keeping the public gaze out. Instead the state could spend that money on the social programs that could potentially render the prison largely obsolete such as youth crime prevention (Griffith University, 2014). The techniques utilised by zoos and aquariums to keep the control of animality hidden from view are largely strategies of marketing and green-washing. By convincing the general public that the captive animal is instead a critical part of some undefined drive to save the species, the zoo or aquarium can claim to fulfil the role of conservationists and species saviours. While perhaps a valid claim, it remains the case that they are nevertheless jailors or the collectors of sentient specimens who will never be permitted to experience life outside of the cage.

Occasionally the punishment of other animals enacted by the state cannot be removed from the public gaze and their torture becomes an unavoidable public spectacle. In July 2020 the Cairns Regional Council (CRC) began to disperse a colony of 8000 endangered spectacled flying foxes from their camp in the Cairns library in the city centre. The weapons used in this dispersal included strobe lights directed at the roosting sites of the spectacled flying foxes, along with loud sounds (shouting, clapping and the loud clapping of pool noodles). As well the CRC used long range acoustic devices (LRAD) directed at the trees and surrounding area to prevent roosting or to lift the animals from the trees (CRC, 2020). LRADs are a sonic weapon commonly used by law enforcement to disperse protest actions. The American Civil

Liberties Union (ACLU) advocates for the removal of LRADs against protests, citing the high potential for acoustic weapons to cause serious and permanent injury, including hearing loss and prolonged ear pain (ACLU, 2020).

Flying foxes of all species frequently come into conflict with human communities due to shared preferences for habitat sites. These conflicts invariably result in negative outcomes for the flying foxes, more so than for the humans. Threats to flying-fox colonies include land clearing for urban development and agriculture, persecution for crop damage and roost site disturbance (Roberts, 2006). Methods for dispersal, including the use of LRADs have been and continue to be equivalent to acts of warfare. As Roberts describes:

> Current methods of disturbing flying foxes include firing "Birdfrite" cartridges, aerosol horns, water spraying, smoke, spotlights, bird of prey calls, gas guns, firecrackers and sometimes even helicopters [...]. Previous attempts to relocate flying-fox colonies have involved shooting, felling or burning roost trees, the use of flame flowers and explosives. (2006, p. 54)

The effects on individuals and whole colonies can be catastrophic. Observer Leni Descalle states she has not only witnessed the separation of pups from mothers, as well as the deaths of adults and young, but a significant psychological change in the flying foxes. In an interview Descalle explains:

> In the early days animals would try to stay and withstand even the most intense and horrific use of sound

and light harassment. Now almost five months later, hundreds of flying foxes can lift [leave the roost] with the smallest of sounds, potentially indicating long-term trauma and increased sensitivity and fear. These animals were very accustomed to loud noise in an urban environment. (2020, Appendix 4)

Exposure to constant loud noise, the use of strobe lights and sleep deprivation were all among techniques of interrogation used against political prisoners held at Guantanamo Bay, according to US Federal Bureau of Investigation (FBI) agents who reported the abuses (Eggen & Smith, 2004). While there are some differences between the sleep cycles of humans when compared to other animals studies have confirmed that no matter the species sleep deprivation is a "potent stressor that leads to metabolic and cognitive disturbances in brain areas involved in learning, memory and emotion" (Alkadhil, Zagaar, Alhaider, Salim & Aleisa, 2013, p. 234).

The flying foxes being dispersed by CRC are literally being subjected to a torture similar to that inflicted upon human political prisoners. The justifications range from public health concerns due to fecal matter and the health of the colony, to the demonisation of the flying foxes as rats with wings, flying cane toads or as the vectors of coronavirus (Descalle, 2020, Appendix 4). The use of speciesist language indicates that the perceived crime of the flying foxes is less to do with their fecal emissions (which can be mitigated through appropriate screening or cleaning policies implemented by a willing local council), and is more to do with the criminality of being an animal living within a human space. The discriminatory logic is that they are not us, and if they cannot assimilate they must be removed irrespective of their inherent rights as sentient individuals. They are dispossessed of their territories and in some cases separated from their young, as the consequences of speciesism continue to advance across the landscape. Bats have become convenient scapegoats for those in the community who do not wish to acknowledge the human role in the emergence of zoonotic disease. Humans continue to seek causes for the COVID-19 pandemic which is arguably a crisis that has emerged from humans' dysfunctional relationship with other animals and the natural world. Even though the flying fox dispersal is highly visible, occurring in the midst of a populated urban space, it can be justified by appealing to the inherent criminality of animality itself and as retribution against a species maligned for the errors of humans.

Perhaps nowhere else is the public display of punishment against the other animal more apparent in daily life than the shelves of the supermarkets and the display cases of the butcher's store. Prior to their closure in 2017, Huon Valley Meat Co. in Hobart chose to hang the bodies of slaughtered pigs in their front windows. This action was part of their marketing campaign that promoted the business as engaging in 'ethical' slaughter (corpses on display convey the message that the business has nothing to hide). The similarities between the inverted shackled corpse of a pig to the dingo nailed to the tree and to the human displayed within the gibbet are manifest.

Even so, the processes which are engaged to create the animal corpse that is hung in the window are for the most part hidden from view. Just as the state will pour money into walls around prisons, so too will the owners of slaughter-houses, feedlots and intensive rearing facilities spend money to hide their operations from view (money which is all too often provided by the state, as discussed in the second essay). The dismembered corpse of the executed animal, cleansed and wrapped in plastic on the supermarket shelf will not inspire the shock or horror felt when confronted by the dingo nailed to a tree or by the still images of Tyke the elephant gunned down in the street. These unseen victims have been strategically de-animalised, the criminality of their very animality exculpated by the slaughterer's knife. The animal is no longer guilty because the animal no longer exists, or rather, the human is no longer guilty of killing because it is not now an animal. As Noske states:

> The body which makes up an important part of the animal 'self' used to be steered largely by the animal itself but has now become like a machine in the hands of management and is actually working against the animal's own interests. (1997, p. 18)

Other animals are alienated from the natural world, they are alienated from the human world and from their own communities. They are even alienated from the products that are wrought from their bodies (Noske, 1997). All that remains is the product and the plastic ear-tag destined for landfill. Very occasionally, glimpses of animality may remain after death and elicit a sense of discomfort. This can occur when the consumer is confronted unexpectedly by a whole suckling pig or the slaughtered fishes with eyes still in situ and mouths agape as though still fighting for breath. This is a momentary shock though, as fleeting as the titillation provided by the death masks of the executed prisoners at Madame Tussauds. They were animals, now they are not. They dared to be animal so humans took away their animality. Through the de-animalisation of other animals, humans reaffirm the physical and ideological spaces necessary to absolve society from any sense of culpability.

It is this need for absolution that drives humans to view other animals as simultaneously being sentient enough to be punished but not sentient enough to be afforded a full range of rights. Humans can justify the deprivations and tortures inflicted upon the other animals' bodies by right of their being aberrations in a human society. In a similar way the criminal human is regarded as an aberration as they are deviant bodies that must be controlled for the good of humankind, and (somewhat paternalistically) must be controlled for their own wellbeing. This is what creates the differentiation between the dog who bites a member of public and the dog owned by police who bites the human described as criminal. The animality of the police dog has been subsumed within the human construct of law and order therefore its expression is not only permitted but actively encouraged. In comparison dogs who are not used by the carceral system who bite exist outside the structure of human law and order must be contained or even destroyed. The wild dog who bites is a criminal while the police dog who bites the criminal is a hero.

When vegans say 'until every cage is empty' we must mean it to its logical conclusion. Not merely as a rhetorical device glibly utilised in advocacy for incarcerated other animals, but as a declaration of intent. It needs to be an active commitment to dismantling the fundamentally unjust carceral system that prevents the realisation of liberation. The relationship between human and other animals is carceral, even in its most benign expressions. Humans cage, punish, torture and execute other animals under the guise of the human advancement. Humans must eat, they must be housed, they must be entertained, the 'cleanliness' of civic spaces must be guaranteed. Other animals will either be made tools to facilitate these human demands or they will be exterminated. As Franklin states:

> Animals figured in the modern project principally as a resource for human progress. The destruction of habitat, the enslavement into medical research and the creation of industrial husbandry regimes were perhaps regrettable to those in the know, but they were always justified through their contribution to the greater (human) good. (1999, p. 3)

It is of fundamental importance that animal advocates recognise the social inequalities that are deliberately constructed by the state and by corporations as a means to continue feeding into the carceral system. The prison industrial complex is inextricably connected to the animal industrial complex in the shared ideological space as well as the very physical realities they both occupy. Until the systems and prisons that incarcerate humans and other animals are deconstructed, including the prisons inside our own heads that make us resistant to change, liberation will continue to elude us all.

References

Alexiou, G. (2020). *No justice, no speech: Autism a deadly hazard when dealing with police.* https://www.forbes.com/sites/gusalexiou/2020/06/14/police-killing-and-criminal-exploitation-dual-threats-to-the-disabled/?sh=74f252a84f0f

Alkadhil, K., Zagaar, M., Alhaider, I., Salim, S., & Aleisa, A. (2013). Neurobiological consequences of sleep deprivation. *Current Neuropharmacology, 11*(3) 231-249. doi: 10.2174/1570159X11311030001

American Civil Liberties Union (2020). *Acoustic weapons fact sheet.* www.aclu.org/fact-sheet/acoustic-weapons-fact-sheet

Best, S. (2014). *The politics of total liberation: Revolution for the 21st century.* Palgrave MacMillan.

Brara, N. (2020). *'This is a revolution': 18 artists from coast to coast share what they saw and felt at the George Floyd protests.* https://news.artnet.com/art-world/artists-protests-george-floyd-testimonials-1876254

Brook, B. (2017). *Bed linen and boomerangs – The surprising products made by prisoners.* https://www.news.com.au/finance/business/other-industries/bed-linen-and-boomerangs-the-surprising-products-made-by-prisoners/news-story/d9cfbb0e9414d00c0ef764ce 8002982

Cairns Regional Council (2020). *Flying-foxes.* https://cairns.qld.gov.au/community-environment/native-animals/flying-foxes

Daly, M. (2013). *Topsy: The startling story of the crooked-tailed elephant, P. T. Barnum, and the American wizard, Thomas Edison*. Atlantic Monthly Press.

Davis, A. (2003). *Are prisons obsolete?* Seven Stories Press.

Eggen, D., & Smith, R. (2004). *FBI agents allege abuse of detainees at Guantanamo Bay*. https://www.washingtonpost.com/archive/politics/2004/12/21/fbi-agents-allege-abuse-of-detainees-at-guantanamo-bay/8fb551bb-ac-4f74-b1c0-3b026e15f68b/

Foucault, M. (1977). *Discipline and punish: The birth of the prison*. Pantheon.

Franklin, A. (1999). *Animals and modern cultures: A sociology of human-animal relation in modernity*. Sage Publications.

Griffith University (2014). *Helping children flourish: Early intervention key to keeping kids out of the criminal justice system*. https://www.griffith.edu.au/research/impact/keeping-children-out-of-prison

Haney, C. (2001). *The psychological impact of incarceration: Implications for post-prison adjustment*. https://www.aspe.hhs.gov/basic-report/psychological-impact-incarceration-implicatons-postprison-adjustment#IV

Hartman, M. (2020). *A new law will allow some California inmates who fight wildfires to have their records expunged*. https://www.marketplace.org/2020/09/16/law-allows-some-california-inmates-firefighters-records-expunged/

Hawaii State Legislature (2018) *H. B. No. 716*. https://www.capitol. hawaii.gov/sessions 2020/bills/HB716_.HTM

Hoover, W. (2004). *Slain elephant left tenuous legacy in animal rights*. http://the. honoluluadvertiser.com/article/2004/Aug/20/ In/In1a.html

Ko, S. (2015). Emphasizing similarities does nothing for the oppressed. In A. Ko & S. Ko (Eds.), *Aphro-ism: Essays on pop culture, feminism, and Black veganism from two sisters* (pp. 37-43). Lantern Books.

Lloyd, M. (2017). *Dead dogs in trees: What's that all about?* https://www.abc. net.au/news/2017-09-03/dead-dogs-why- are-they-being-strung-up-on-trees/8867584

Mascall, K. (2020). Interview 11/11/2020. *See Appendix 4.*

McMillan, F. (2017). Behavioural and psychological outcomes for dogs sold as puppies through pet stores and/or born in commercial breeding establishments: Current knowledge and putative causes. *Journal of Veterinary Behavior, 19*, 14-26.

Nitsche, H. (2020). *The orgies mysteries theatre*. https://www. nitsch.org/en/aktionen

Noske, B. (1997). *Beyond boundaries: Humans and animals*. Black Rose Books.

Pliny the Elder (1991). *Natural history: A selection*. John F. Healy (Trans.), Penguin Books.

Mapping Police Violence (2020). *National Trends*. https:// mappingpoliceviolence.org/nationaltrends

Rauby, B., & Kopf, D. (2015). *Prisons of poverty: Uncovering the pre-incarceration incomes of the imprisoned.* https://prisonpolicy.org/reports/income.html

Roberts, B. (2006). *Management of urban flying-fox camps: Issues of relevance to camps in the lower Clarence, NSW.* Valley Watch Inc., MacClean.

Schroeder, J. (2009). *The day they hanged Mary the elephant in Tennessee.* https://blueridgecountry.com/archive/favorites/mary-the-elephant

Seidman, S. (2016). *Contested knowledge: Social theory today* (5th ed.). Wiley-Blackwell.

Singer, P. (2009). *Animal liberation* (updated ed.). Harper Collins Publishers.

Thompson, N. (2018). *Promoting equality: Working with diversity and difference.* Palgrave Macmillan.

Vegan Life (2017). *Black vegans rock-Aph Ko talks about her remarkable work.* https://www.veganlifemag.com/black-vegans-rock/

Wadiwel, D. (2015). *The War Against Animals.* Koninklijke Brill.

Weir, K. (2012). Alone in 'the hole': Psychologists probe the mental health effects of solitary confinement. *American Psychological Association, 42*(5), 54.

Wyckoff, J. (2015). Analysing animality: A critical approach. *The Philosophical Quarterly, 65*(260), 529-546.

Breaking the web:
Strategies and tactics
for animal advocates

Activism as a tool for social change relies heavily upon effective public relations. The successful dissemination of a liberatory message is largely determined by how accepting the broader public is of that message (Werder, 2006). This necessitates an analysis as to whether the current strategies employed by animal advocates and the vegan movement are proving effective. An investigation is provided into new and perhaps underutilised methods including nonviolent civil disobedience. This is more essential than ever as the social space has altered globally due to the pandemic crisis that has restricted engagement with the more traditional activist strategies (such as street outreach or slaughterhouse vigils).

Thus far in this work I have provided philosophical, historical and political investigations into those systems that comprise the animal industrial complex. Now I will investigate alternatives to animal advocates' reliance upon street outreach, vigils and marches. Australian government responses to COVID-19 have caused the closure of national and state borders and the increasing restrictions of movement within the public space. In turn, this has subsequently revealed the failures inherent within activism that relies upon travel and mass mobilisation. The rising numbers of other animals being slaughtered annually highlights the weaknesses of street outreach to inform the public of the realities of their consumer choices within the misguided capitalist framework of supply and demand. Further, the activism of groups such as (but not exclusively) Anonymous for the Voiceless and The Save Movement has been noticeably curtailed during the pandemic. Additionally, over the years, some individuals and entire groups have moved away from these activism structures while simultaneously levelling criticisms based upon the inequities of hierarchy, populism and colonialism manifest within these global movements (Truth of Cube, 2018). Activism seems to be stagnating.

Clearly a change of both strategy and tactic is required. There are four key under-utilised tactics and strategies that I will investigate here; divestment, brandalism, blockade and mutual aid. These investigations are offered with the understanding that the diversification of tactics should not and does not end here. I will offer some suggestions on engagement with these tactics where appropriate. I also suggest a fifth strategy that can change the world one individual at a time when they contribute to other animal liberation by going vegan.

It is undeniable that animal advocacy and vegans are more visible today than they ever have been. There seems to be more vegans, more plant-based options, more consistent media and corporate exposure and more activism and online content than in preceding years. According to Google trends, searches for veganism increased sevenfold from 2014 to 2018 with more people looking up veganism than vegetarianism or gluten-free (The Vegan Society, 2018). Fast food chains proudly display the word vegan on new product lines, vegan social media groups are dominated by discussions of food and products. Documentaries and feature films relating to veganism and animal rights have made their way onto mainstream viewing platforms (for example, The Game Changers (2018) and Okja (2017), both on Netflix). Yet vegans seem to have drifted from the original roots of veganism from the vision of Watson (1944) and Cross (1954). This is evident in that most mainstream vegans and celebri-vegans struggle to acknowledge (or vociferously reject) the inherently political nature of veganism.

In recent years, animal advocates have relied upon an apolitical 'go vegan' appeal to the masses, relying upon the hope that planting seeds through outreach and exposés will somehow result in the creation of a vegan utopia. The assumption was that the liberation of other animals from human exploitation will ostensibly arise from consumer demand products that are promoted as being more ethical.

Through connections online and in person, the company animal advocates keep and the names and brands followed, they may feel confident of the great vegan future but it can also isolate vegans from the broader community. It appears that vegans have effectively created a constraining web around themselves as individuals and as a movement. This limits the movement's social capital and collective ability to affect broad scale change and draws animal advocates further into the animal and related industrial complexes. The vegan movement's rhetoric of winning against the animal industrial complex has been shown in preceding essays to be manifestly untrue.

Ornelas (2019) of the Food Empowerment Project has articulated her discomfort with global chapter-based activism organisations due to their replication of colonisation. According to Hovarth (1972) colonisation is the process through which a settler group migrates to a region separate from the original coloniser state. The colonisers occupy the country and establish physical colonies whilst creating lasting systems of dominance over local populations through forced assimilation or, in some cases, extermination of people and culture (Hovarth, 1972). Animal advocates and other activist groups, predominantly from the Global North, travel throughout the world including to countries in the Global South. They establish chapters that subsume local grassroots activism into a mode of activism that may not be suitable to the region or culture. Prior to the global pandemic, activist tours were commonplace, with a select handful of individuals granted financial sponsorship to travel the world. Their mission was to influence local activism scenes with a blueprint created in an entirely different region or cultural group in a manner not dissimilar to a religious missionary (Ornelas, 2019). Ornelas (2019) argues that when colonisers enter other countries they change how people eat, the expression of their culture, and their languages. In a similar way, when activist groups' chapters are established by organisations from dominant English-speaking countries (the Global North), local activists in non-English speaking countries (the Global South) are expected to adopt English in the naming of the chapter, even if they utilise their own language in posts on social media or during activist events (Ornelas, 2019). Further, these imposed "chapters are stifling this movement, are restricting creativity, [and] they are limiting what we can do as activists" (Ornelas, 2019, n.p.).

There are consequences for a reliance upon limited modes of activism dictated by a handful of individuals and the expectation that chapters across the world must abide by a single tactic or code of behaviour. One consequence is that these actions can divert resources and people away from projects that could be more effective, dependent upon the culture or region in which the activists are operating. Activist groups cannot replicate a tactic ad nauseum and expect that it will work universally, even within their own countries and communities. This is not a phenomenon unique to the modern vegan movement. Voskoboynik (2018) discusses how 19th century colonial views of conservation and ecology were further opportunities for colonial control over Indigenous populations, as entire natural spaces were enclosed for their 'protection.' Colonisation practices of this type enclose the social activism space within a framework that excludes local communities from the full autonomous expression of their identities and cultural connection. This can create hierarchies and potentially systems of domination in a movement that is supposed to be striving to deconstruct those exact systems. Activist groups in other animal liberation cannot afford to perpetuate coloniser models of activism through which a select few individuals are granted the role of missionaries to increase the power base of an organisation. Not only is it proving ineffective, it is unethical and inconsistent with the aims of the animal rights and broader vegan movement.

Adapt or die — this is a message that the animal rights movement must take to heart. Adopting a range of tactics and strategies that target myriad facets of the oppressive systems is paramount for the movement to move forwards and affect the political, industrial and institutional changes necessary for the actualisation of animal liberation. Animal advocates can no longer depend upon the promise of winning, nor on the need to feel like they are doing something with no critical analysis of the structure or consequences of that something. A concerted, informed and collective effort is needed to break the web of intersecting oppressions, including those of animal advocates' own making which can inadvertently perpetuate colonising and, hence, oppressive practices. To that end, there is much to be gained by engaging in critical dialogue as suggested by the preceding essays. Alongside this is the opportunity to investigate new or under-utilised forms of activism, and thereby, to entirely reimagine the social spaces for humans and other animals.

Animal advocacy strategy of divestment

Divestment campaigns target institutions including banks, superannuation funds and educational institutions, demanding responsible investing practices. This can be achieved through the selection of ethical projects or corporations to invest in or, more commonly, by the decision to no longer actively invest in unethical projects or corporations. The strategy is part of a global initiative to effect social change through ethical financial and insurance businesses called Socially Responsible Investing (SRI) which "aims to balance out the power of the purely money-profit-driven market" (Bakshi, 2013, p. 248). Bakshi (2013) explains that the push for SRI derives from global concerns about the impact of climate change and social unrest. Concern for other animals' wellbeing can be included in the motivating influences of SRI.

As a tactic, divestment falls within an overall strategy that aims to influence corporate decision-making through pressure campaigning, by targeting their profit margins as well as their social licence. Social licence refers to the community's ability to withdraw its tacit support for an industry or product which can affect corporate reputation and profitability (Brueckner & Ross, 2020). Divestment campaigns work. According to the Go Fossil Free (GFF) divestment commitment tracker the value of institutions divesting or committing to divest from fossil fuels is worth over \$14.48 trillion (Go Fossil Free, 2020). Divestment remains relatively underutilised within the animal rights movement. However, it represents an opportunity to not only generate discussion regarding the role of banks in directly funding animal exploitation, but also to potentially disrupt the financial relationships upon which the animal industrial complex is reliant.

Many financial institutions have vague animal welfare statements that claim to uphold the basic "five freedoms" of animal welfare (Royal Society for the Prevention of Cruelty to Animals (RSPCA), 2009). The five freedoms are: freedom from hunger and thirst; from discomfort; from pain, injury or disease; from fear and distress, and; to express normal behaviour (RSPCA, 2009). The respected animal welfare agency encourages their clients in the animal agriculture industries to adhere to those guidelines. The RSPCA's (2009) document represents a dominant view of welfare towards other animals. It is thereby implicated in an instrumentalist view of other animals as shown by language such as "humane killing" and "animal management" (RSPCA, 2009). This is an example of contradictory values in a mainstream pro-animal organisation.

Most financial institutions do not stipulate a legally binding adherence to the animal welfare guidelines as part of their lending policies. The Commonwealth Bank has no public statement or policy at all. A few financial institutions have stipulated projects that they will not actively fund. For example:

ING Bank (2020) will not fund businesses involved with:

- Animal fighting for entertainment
- Commercial trade in endangered species
- Fur farms, or the trade/manufacture of fur
- Testing on animals for cosmetics
- Use of non-human primates or endangered/threatened species for testing.

National Australia Bank (NAB) (2020) will not fund businesses involved with:

- Animal fighting for entertainment
- Trade in endangered/threatened species except for conservation
- Fur farms, or the trade/manufacture of fur from endangered species
- Testing on animals for cosmetics
- Use of non-human primates or endangered/threatened species for testing
- Shark finning
- Commercial whaling
- Destructive fishing practices such as poisoning or explosives.

Westpac Bank (2020) will not fund businesses involved with:

- Shark finning
- Commercial whaling.

Despite appearing to be progressive on the surface, these statements and policies are guidelines to be applied according to the discretion of the lender. Many claims look good on paper but in fact retain loopholes such as trading in endangered animals for the purposes of conservation. This can involve the incarceration, breeding and exploitation of other animals for commercial purposes in zoos and aquariums, many of whom hide behind green-washing campaigns to justify their commercial activities. For example, Zoodoo located in Tasmania has been involved in the captive breeding of white lions, ostensibly as part of a global conservation effort to preserve the species (Kempton, 2014). This is despite the fact that whilst white lions are a rare genetic mutation of the tawny lions they are in fact not a distinct subspecies (Schofield, 2013). The lions who have been bred at Zoodoo will not be released to boost the populations in the wild. Rather, they were removed from their mothers at merely four weeks of age for handrasing and will remain in captivity for life as part of the zoos public encounters (Conway, 2014). None of these activities are excluded under the animal welfare policies set out by the major Australian lenders. It should be noted that none of Australia's banks explicitly exclude intensive farming practices, feedlots or live export. According to Animals Australia, three financial institutions alone (NAB, ANZ and Commonwealth Bank) collectively fund over 80% of live exports in Australia (Animals Australia, 2020). It should be noted that the Commonwealth Bank has not committed to a defined animal welfare policy at this time.

In March 2020 Animals Australia launched their Banking on Cruelty campaign which encouraged signatories to question their banks on their animal welfare policies. They were asked to demand their financial institutions divest from animal exploitation industries including the live export trade. At the time of writing nearly 20 000 individuals have signed onto the campaign (Animals Australia, 2020). The campaign was met with some apprehension by producers, especially within the live export sector where there were reports of some lenders denying bank accounts and loans to businesses involved in the scandal-wracked industry. Mark Harvey-Sutton, the CEO of the Australian Livestock Exporters Association (ALEC) said financial institutions withholding lending "does not promote or support the industry and the genuine care producers, exporters and importers have for the animals in the supply chains" (Nason, 2020, n.p.). More tellingly, however, he stated that banks acceding to demands for animal welfare policies in banking were "just creating further business models for animal activist organisations" (Nason, 2020, n.p.). His words should be taken as encouragement for future actions of this nature.

If one campaign targeting financial industries can provoke this concern from an industry lobbyist, imagine what a number of ongoing and consistent campaigns targeting national and international financial institutions could achieve. The good news is divestment campaigns are relatively simple to create and provide an opportunity for activists to step into the broader community as community members, rather than creating conflict with the vegan community. Some steps citizens can take are:

- Research the financial institutions in your area, including providers of superannuation and find out if they have an animal welfare policy or statement.

- Find the loopholes in the statement, working out what business activities will or will not be financed by the financial institution.

- Begin publicising the policy guidelines, creating a petition addressed to the financial institution demanding they cease funding or investing in projects that exploit other animals, including intensive farming or live export.

- Provide members of the public with the information they need to remove their business from financial institutions who fail to acknowledge their demands.

- Publicise, publicise, publicise; the more people who sign onto your campaign, the greater the disruption to the financial networks upon which banks and industry rely.

Remember to centre the campaign on animal rights by making sure the language and information provided avoids inadvertently sanctioning the continued involvement of financial institutions (or the signatories to your petition) in funding animal exploitation.

Animal advocacy strategy of ad-hacking and brandalism
The public realm is dominated by an onslaught of corporate advertising which occupies almost every viable space including billboards, public transport and bus shelters. These visual spaces are bought and occupied by companies in what can be viewed as another manifestation of the enclosure of the visual commons by corporate entities. As anti-speciesist activist group Smash Speciesism states:

> They never asked us for permission, we never asked them either. Advertisement must be the single most in-your-face tool that capitalism uses. And the world is littered with it. From bus stops to huge billboards, public space is stolen from us to force us into the trading submission that keeps the world rolling. It isn't just horrible speciesist advertisements that litter the world. Plant based adverts are growing, and even so called anti-speciesist groups BUY advertisements to tell people to "go vegan", like veganism was a thing you could achieve simply by consuming plant based products. We don't care what the message is. Paying money to advertisement companies to upkeep their social brainwashing is unacceptable. We are fucking done with it. Those spaces are not for a business to sell, nor are they there for a company to buy, regardless of their message. (2020c, n.p.)

Ad-hacking and brandalism is a form of nonviolent direct action that reclaims the public space from advertising companies and corporate entities by removing their advertising and replacing it with subversive messaging. Quite surprisingly, it has something of an extensive history as a form of activism in Australia. In 1979, Bill Snow began a graffiti campaign targeting billboard advertising for tobacco in Sydney. His initiative led to the creation of Billboard Utilising Graffitists Against Unhealthy Promotions (BUGA-UP). Soon artists were targeting not only tobacco companies but also alcohol promotions and Coca Cola. The movement counted doctors, political economists and university professors amongst its founders and members. It included people not otherwise associated with radical protest graffiti. Yet they are credited with having influenced the public discourse surrounding Big Tobacco that eventually led to a ban on tobacco advertising in Australia in 1991 (Lambert, 2018). The BUGA-UP website is still active to this day with a 'How To' section encouraging individuals to engage in subverting corporate advertising with nothing more than a spray can and the desire to make a change (BUGA-UP, 2018).

There have been multiple campaigns utilising the tactics of replacing advertising with subversive messaging since the inception of BUGA-UP. There are campaigns that provide social commentary on contemporary issues and create important public dialogue. They also have the potential to cost advertising agencies and their clients significant amounts of money in replacing or repairing advertisements and through lost advertising itself. The following are recent examples:

- Bushfire Brandalism (Australia): In February 2020 the Bushfire Brandalism campaign saw 41 artists replace 78 advertising posters in Sydney, Melbourne and Brisbane, to provide commentary on the devastating bushfires that had swept across the country and the climate crisis that had contributed to their severity. The activist group Brandalism states:

As a collective group of Australian artists, we have been driven to reclaim public advertising space with posters speaking to the Australian government's inaction on climate change and the devastating bushfires. We do not accept that this situation is 'business as usual'. We are making these issues visible in our public spaces and in our media; areas monopolized by entities maintaining conservative climate denial agendas. If the newspapers won't print the story, we will! (2020, n.p.)

Many of the images were focused on the impacts of the bushfires upon other animal communities such as the devastation wrought upon the already decimated koala populations. It also included Quick Response (QR) barcodes that linked the public to charity organisations working directly on the issue. The campaign organisers also questioned the role of the media in reporting on the climate crisis, citing concentrated media ownership as a factor in the undermining of climate crisis information.

- Smash Speciesism (UK): Unidentified members of UK-based anti-speciesism group Smash Speciesism engaged in a brandalism campaign in August 2020. It involved replacing multiple advertising posters in bus shelters (including advertising by McDonalds) with their own. The messages on the new posters included "call in sick and block a slaughterhouse" and "wear a face covering and smash a butcher's shop". These statements provide commentary on: the capitalist system which compels individuals to work in order to consume; the role of corporate advertising to promote the consumption of other animals, as well as; the importance of anonymity (through the wearing of face masks) in activism, all set within an unapologetically anti-speciesist framework.

- Product stickering campaigns (global): The stickering of supermarket products with animal rights messaging has been widely reported by the media in recent years. Stickers may include health warnings relating to the consumption of other animal products, whilst others directly focus on the cruelty inherent in the exploitation of other animals. The use of QR codes linking the purchaser of the products to online footage exposing the reality of how that product was manufactured also became popular in 2018. Multiple news articles have reported on sticker activism with many people expressing shock or anger at being 'meat-shamed.' The method effectively provides a platform that shares the message further than just the supermarket. One Woolworths manager claimed such stickering is a regular occurrence with 10-20 products routinely targeted by stickering (including dairy, eggs and meat products) and staff regularly having to remove them from products. A spokesperson for the supermarket giant stated they would deal with the "deliberate vandalism of products seriously" (Bungard, 2019, n.p.).

Subverting the corporate advertising space has been utilised effectively to force necessary dialogues into the public sphere. In doing so it provides an economical and efficient method of activism for those who are willing to push the boundaries of the law in order to advocate for other animals and reclaim the commons from enclosure by capitalism.

Animal advocacy strategies of facility lockdowns, occupations, open rescues

Lockdowns and occupations of facilities where the exploitation of other animals is perpetrated have been utilised as a tactic to raise public awareness, negotiate the release of other animals where possible and cause economic disruption to businesses for decades. Open rescue as a tactic was pioneered in Australia by Patty Mark in 1993 and involves activists entering facilities without concealing their identities. From the early 1980s Pam "The Chook Woman" Clarke was facilitating the liberation of hens from Tasmanian battery farms. She was still involved in midnight raids until the early 2000s. Actions such as open rescues, blockades including vigils and physical occupations are now facilitated by ready access to social media as a means to broadcast images and footage from inside these facilities to the world. It can have the effect of undermining public confidence in the industries they support. Those who engage in these actions with the intent to obstruct the operations of facilities recognise that there is limited scope to affect the immediate cessation of animal exploitation via these tactics. However, the economic disruptions caused (and acknowledged by facility owners and operations) are regularly touted as indicators of a successful action. Notable cases are:

- Luv-a-Duck, Nhill (2018): A six-hour occupation of a duck slaughterhouse resulting in the liberation of 20 ducks, an action that CEO Darryl Bussel stated caused economic losses in the tens of thousands due to lost productivity and the need to implement increased security measures (Legislative Council Economy and Infrastructure Committee, 2019a).

- Tulip Pork, Manchester, UK (2019): A fourteen-hour lock-down outside the slaughterhouse utilising arm-lock devices positioned in the driveway of the facility, organised by Smash Speciesism. It reportedly resulted in economic losses to the total of £158 000 ($287 000 AUD). A repeat action at the facility later in the year, by Animal Rebellion, is reported to have cost the facility the same amount, resulting in losses of over half a million dollars for one company in one year. (Smash Speciesism 2020a; Smash Speciesism 2020b).

- Diamond Valley Egg Farm (2019): Activists investigating and rescuing hens from the egg farm were accused of breaching biosecurity during a salmonella outbreak, which was not proven. However the controls the company had to implement following the rescue activity resulted in the loss of revenue for over 12 months, additional security measures, the loss of contracts both domestic and export, and the requirement to pay out staff who qualified for redundancies (Legislative Council Economy and Infrastructure Committee, 2019b).

These are a mere handful of examples of actions that have obstructed the ability of animal exploitation facilities to engage in their daily operations. According to Victoria Police, 11 instances of protest and 11 instances of trespass relating to protest at farms and slaughterhouses were reported between May 2018 to May 2019 (Severs, 2019). Groups of individuals organised under the banners of Meat the Victims, Farm Transparency Project (formerly Aussie Farms), Direct Action Everywhere, various Save chapters and assorted other independent groups or collectives, have all engaged in facility occupations and lockdowns worldwide, potentially resulting in economic damages in the millions. That is the heart of these industries, the profitability of animal exploitation is targeted by the activists. Disrupting businesses through their operational costs and the additional security requirements that often become a necessity for businesses to invest in, can prove an effective strategy in many cases, though the exact figures may be difficult to calculate.

Animal advocacy strategy of mutual aid networks

When Kropotkin (1914) defined his understanding of mutual aid in *Mutual aid: A factor of evolution*, it was based on the observations he had made of other animals in the natural world. This was no Disney-fied representation of the wilderness, instead it was the understanding that where other animals strive against one another within their species groups then progress as a population or as a species is inhibited. Kropotkin writes:

> On the other hand, wherever I saw animal life in abundance, as, for instance, on the lakes where scores of species and millions of individuals came together to rear their progeny; in the colonies of rodents; in the migrations of birds which took place at that time on a truly American scale along the Usuri; and especially in a migration of fallow-deer which I witnessed on the Amur, and during which scores of thousands of these intelligent animals came together from an immense territory, flying before the coming deep snow, in order to cross the Amur where it is narrowest — in all these scenes of animal life which passed before my eyes, I saw Mutual Aid and Mutual Support carried on to an extent which made me suspect in it a feature of the greatest importance for the maintenance of life, the preservation of each species, and its further evolution. (1914, p. xii)

Mutual aid is a system of social participation in which each individual bears the responsibility for the other, creating support networks and new forms of infrastructure and community networks. It is an interspecies capacity which draws attention to the diversity of ways other animals and non-sentient beings have agency in the making of the world (Willett, 2014). It contrasts with a corporatised version of charity which has effectively commodified the exploitation of vulnerable individuals and groups including other animals and impoverished communities. Mutual aid is a dedication to performing certain acts of assistance that will help others towards self-determination and autonomy. It opens the door for understanding how:

> A trans-species ethical commitment will involve fostering interspecies ways of relating that dislodge the individual, human subject from the top of species hierarchy to learn with, be with and co-create with our kin [other animals and non-human beings] a common liveable world. (Ross, Bennett & Menyweather, 2021, p. 182)

How could mutual aid manifest amongst the vegan and animal rights movements? Food Not Bombs has been providing meals to houseless individuals and attendees at protest actions. They have also fulfilled the role of first responders to communities impacted by natural disasters, since 1980. All the food is vegan (or at the very least vegetarian) and mostly made from donated goods (by the public or local businesses) or salvaged products thus removing the necessity to support global food monopolies. After Hurricane Katrina decimated New Orleans in 2005, scott crow (he prefers not to capitalise his name) established The Common Ground Collective, a decentralised group of non-for-profit organisations that eventually provided more community aid to affected residents than The Red Cross, and their work included other animals (Conroy, 2020). This work eventuated in the illegal construction of a community medical centre to serve local disadvantaged people (Conroy, 2020). Over the past few years Elizabeth Jones, founder of Operation Liberation, has been entering disaster zones with a dedicated team to rescue other animals from flood waters and storm damaged regions. They provide veterinary care to stray and rescued animals, reuniting many with their families if possible or removing them from the area to be rehabilitated, fostered and safely rehomed, whilst document-ing the atrocities inflicted upon other animals abandoned to die on farms during natural disasters.

Other manifestations of human initiated mutual aid networks include:

- Prisoner support for arrested or imprisoned activists: making sure there are people on standby to collect arrested activists from police stations, to attend court days, covering legal costs for each other, or writing and sending supplies to political prisoners.

- Childcare collectives that would enable parents of children to engage in activism and create strong community connections between families and carers.

- Safehouse networks to hide activists from both the law and from potentially violent individuals from the animal exploitation industries.

- The provision of training in the legal rights of activists, on de-escalation tactics or on strategies to de-arrest activists at actions.

- The establishment of no-cost travelling veterinary services for other animals living in marginalised communities.

- Non-corporate foodbanks redistributing donated and salvaged plant-based goods to the community, assisting others to not have to rely on the purchase of animal-based products from global food monopolies.

- Library collectives sharing works on the political theories that provide frameworks for activism, paired with book discussion groups through which those ideas can be discussed and made accessible to all.

- Free plant-based health and nutrition courses, with access to recipes and how to cook them, empowering communities towards optimum health (within a body positivity and a culturally sensitive framework).

- The establishment of community gardens with access to produce to feed communities and as a means to impart knowledge so communities can become self-sufficient and sustainable.

This list is by no means exhaustive, the possibilities for mutual aid are limitless. As scott crow states:

> Whereas if we started to build resilient communities and larger infrastructure, liberatory infrastructure, and I don't mean only fucking non-profits or cooperative businesses. I mean infrastructure that meets basic needs: health care, education, food systems, child care, elderly care, all the foundations of civil society, so that when the next disaster erupts we already have networks that people can plug into [...]. (cited in Black, 2017, n.p.)

The relevance of mutual aid is in its ability to create the strong communities needed to face crises whether the crises are climate related, or a pandemic, or in the struggle for liberation of humans, other animals and the Earth. A central tenet of mutual aid is the requirement to ask individuals and communities what they need and to listen to them. Self-determination is a fundamental freeing principle, including when interacting with other animals. If aid is rendered to individuals of another species, as far as it is practicable their autonomy must be respected. If communities expressing need are entered, their needs and wishes must be respected. In both cases their experiences of suffering and oppression must not be tokenised in pursuit of clout via social media. Mutual aid is not inclusive of saviourism or self-aggrandisement and is not mutual if oppression is occurring.

Animal advocate strategy – Go Vegan!

This may seem an unusual suggestion for a strategic action, given the preceding chapters that have highlighted the significant flaws in the mainstream vegan message. However, practicable veganism, whilst by no means perfect, offers the non-vegan animal advocate, and non-vegans in general, the means to extricate themselves from socio-political systems of exploitation as far as is possible in the current times. As discussed in the second essay, veganism affords all animal-advocates avenues to become ethically consistent. Thus actions undertaken in solidarity with other animals cease to be selectively based upon arbitrary distinctions of species, and instead become part of a holistic recognition of other animal autonomy and sentience. Whilst vegan consumerism may not be yielding the results we may have hoped for, this is no excuse for continuing to perpetuate harms against other animals that are avoidable, whether for personal tastes or corporate profits. And where veganism cannot be practicably applied we must strive for systemic change. This can manifest through support for individuals or organisations who are seeking to revolutionise food systems, technological and medical systems, or political systems. Veganism as an ethical standpoint cannot be discounted as a fundamentally important strategy in pursuit of justice for other animals, for humans and for the Earth.

The above tactics and strategies encompass but a handful of possibilities, some easier to engage in and less confrontational than others. Certainly beginning the move to veganism is something all individuals are able to commit now. I must stress that where I have listed tactics that cross the line of the law, I am not encouraging individuals or organisations to engage in illegal behaviour. Rather, I am investigating their usage by some and the efficacy of those actions. It is a principle of nonviolence theory that only as much force or pressure as is necessary should be used to resist violent and dangerous situations (O'Toole, 2013). This is based on the right to self defence. Thus, I would encourage the reader to further consider the role strategic civil disobedience and other nonviolent direct actions have played in the pursuit of justice (Sharp, 2005). Examples are those disruptive and often confrontational actions of the civil rights movement (including the modern Black Lives Matter movement), the anti-war movement, as well as myriad other social justice movements who used civil disobedience as a means to effect broad scale change.

At the core of the aforementioned examples lies a need to step beyond the echo chamber of a mainstream iteration of veganism that is dependent upon social media and consumerism. It is vital to actively create and facilitate projects that foster connections within human and other animal communities rather than placing the activist in conflict with those communities. It remains the case nevertheless, that an over preoccupation with 'in house' ethics within the vegan movement, while important for its members' integrity as leaders, can take the focus off the animal industrial complex. It is the elites of the government and industry who profit from the exploitation of other animals often in tandem with marginalised humans (Ross, 2020), who require the main scrutiny and challenging on as many fronts as possible. Systems of oppression are held in place by people who gain from the status quo. This being a relevant point of reflection to avoid a scenario of becoming overwhelmed by a seemingly monolithic, bigger than humans and bigger than activists' influence in oppressive situations (Leonard, 1997).

What must be considered next is whether the activist identity itself is an obstruction to creating community which may prove the hardest web of all for us to escape from.

References

Animals Australia (2020). *How does your bank measure up when it comes to animal welfare?* https://www.animalsaustralia.org/features/bank-measure-up-animal-welfare.php

Bakshi, R. (2013). Empathy and transformation: The search for well-being and justice after Gandhi. In J. Sethia & A. Narayan (Eds.), *The living Gandhi: Lessons for our times* (pp. 241-255). Penguin Books.

Black, L. (2017). *The feeling is mutual: Interview with scott crow.* https://www.pmpress.org/blog /2019/07/24/the-feeling-is-mutual-interview-with-scott-crow

Brandalism (2020). *Bushfire brandalism.* http://brandalism.ch.projects/bushfire/

Billboard Utilising Graffitists Against Unhealthy Promotion, BUGA-UP (1980). *B.U.G.A. U.P. beginnings.* https://www.bugaup.org/publications-1980.htm

Bungard, M. (2019). *'Cancer and erectile dysfunction': Vegan activists target supermarkets.* https://www.smh.com.au/national/nsw/cancer-and-erectile-dysfunction-vegan-activists-target-supermarkets-20190319-p515fr.html

Brueckner, M., & Ross, D. (2020). Eco-activism and social work: In the public interest. In D. Ross, M. Brueckner, M. Palmer & W. Eaglehawk (Eds.), *Eco-activism & social work: New directions in leadership and group work* (pp. 3-25). Routledge.

Conroy, J. (2020). *scott crow: Created more mutual aid than the Red Cross*. https://youtu.be/sh38ECkw6zl

Conway, B. (2014). *Lion cubs at Zoodoo Wildlife Park revealed to the public*. https://www. vegantasmania.com/2014/01/lion-cubs-at-zoodoo-wildlife-park-revealed-to-the-public

Go Fossil Free (2020). *1000+ divestment commitments*. https://gofossilfree.org/divestment/commitments

Hovarth, K. (1972). Definition of colonialism. *Current Anthropology, 13*(1), 45-57.

ING Banking (2020). *Animal welfare*. https://www.ing.com/Sustainability/Our-Stance/Animal-welfare.htm

Kempton, H. (2014). *Zoodoo's white lion cubs now almost four months old*. https://www.the mercury.com.au/news/tasmania/zoodoos-white-lion-cubs-now-almost-four-months-old/news-story/e734d0eedebe16d87f4d39ba46da285c

Kropotkin, P. (1914). *Mutual aid: A factor of evolution*. Dover Publications.

Lambert, J. (2018). *How satirists with spray cans defeated big tobacco*. https://www.medical republic.com.au/satirists-spray-cans-defeated-big-tobacco/

Legislative Council Economy and Infrastructure Committee (2019a). *Inquiry into the impact of animal rights activism on animal agriculture: Luv-a-Duck*. https://www.parliament.vic.gov.au/images/stories/committees/SCEI/Animal_rights_activism/transcripts/4._FINAL-AA-Luv-a-Duck.pdf

Legislative Council Economy and Infrastructure Committee (2019b). *Inquiry into the impact of animal rights activism on animal agriculture: Diamond Valley Eggs.* https://www.parliament.vic.gov.au/images/stories/committees/SCEI/Animal_rights_activism/Submissions/S228_-_Diamond_Valley_Egg_Farm_Redacted.pdf

Leonard, P. (1997). *Postmodern welfare: Reconstructing the emancipatory project.* Sage Publications.

Nason, J. (2020). *Don't bow to 'radical activism', rural leaders urge banks.* https://www.beefcentral.com/news/rural-groups-urge-banks-not-to-bow-to-activism/

National Australia Bank (NAB). (2019). *Animal welfare principles.* https://www.news.nab.com.au/news_room_posts/supporting-sustainability-in-the-agriculture-industry/

Ornelas, L. (2019). *Reclaiming our grassroots.* https://youtu.be/1adQt7UPr8I

O'Toole, J. (2013). The practical idealist: Gandhi's leadership lessons. In T. Sethia & A. Narayan (Eds.), *The living Gandhi: Lessons of our time* (pp. 141-162). Penguin Books.

Ross, D. (2020). *The revolutionary social worker: The love ethic model.* Brisbane: Revolutionaries.

Ross, D., Bennett, B., & Menyweather, N. (2021). Towards a critical posthumanist social work: Trans-species ethics of ecological justice, nonviolence and love. In B. Pease & V. Bozalek (Eds.). *Post-anthropocentric social work: Critical posthumanism and new materialist perspectives* (pp. 175-186). Routledge.

Schofield, A. (2013). *White lion: Back to the wild*. Quickfox Publishing.

Severs, J. (2019). *Farmers encouraged to give voice to inquiry*. https://www.dairynews australia.com.au/news/2019/09/25/794339/farmers-urged-to-give-voice-to-inquiry

Sharp, G. (2005). *Waging nonviolence struggle: 20th century practice and 21st century potential*. Extending Horizons Books.

Smash Speciesism (2020a). *Together we can really fuck shit up*. https://www.facebook.com/111830106849525/posts/199994534699748/

Smash Speciesism (2020b). We shut down Tulip! https://www.facebook.com/story.php?story_fbid=343197080379492&id=111830106849525

Smash Speciesism (2020c). *Antispeciesism action*. https://www.facebook.com/111830106849525/posts/332423878123479/

The Royal Society for the Prevention of Cruelty to Animals (2009). *Five freedoms for animals*. http://kb.rspca.org.au/Five-freedoms-for-animals_318.html

The Vegan Society (2018). *Statistics*. https://www.vegansociety.com/news/media/statistics

Truth of Cube (2018). *Truth of Cube: Compilation of evidence*. https://drive.google.com/file/d/17_3_ENIUXWyQ5GmK76k4ZUzxyW0hGTDN/view

Voskoboynik, D. (2018). *The memory we could be: Overcoming fear to create our ecological future*. New Society Publishers.

Werder, K. (2006). Responding to activism: An experimental analysis of public relations strategy influence on attributes of publics. *Journal of Public Relations Research, 18*(4), 335-56.

Westpac Bank (2020). *Agribusiness position statement.* https://www.westpac.com.au/about-westpac/sustainability/our-positions-and-perspectives/

Willett, C. (2014). *Interspecies ethics.* Columbia University Press.

The activist identity must die

I have been involved in animal advocacy and activism since early 2011, which incidentally was before I adopted veganism. My earliest forays into advocacy centred on the rescue, rehabilitation and rehoming for puppies, rabbits, guinea pigs, cats and the occasional rooster. It was not uncommon for my husband to return home from work to find a feathered creature on the couch, or some new furred companion already occupying his side of the bed. To be truthful, this hasn't changed much over the years. In 2012 I established an independent self-funded organisation, Dilly Dally Rabbit Rescue, which ran until 2017. It was through rabbit rescue that I first became aware of the horrors of rabbit farming and thus engaged in my first ever undercover investigation of an animal exploitation facility. Together with a number of foster carers and adoptive homes, my rescue group successfully rehabilitated and rehomed hundreds of rabbits. Every year since, my immersion into the world of advocacy and activism has intensified. In 2016 I was asked to join the committee for Animal Liberation Tasmania and I was approached to establish a Save chapter in late 2017. I have organised and joined multiple actions including vigils and facility occupations, and I have been invited to appear as a speaker at multiple festivals and protest actions across Australia.

Suffice to say, I've done more than some and much less than others. What my experiences in activism and exposure to people within this and other social justice movements has given me is a burning desire to do better. Not just as an individual, but as part of a movement. Sadly what I have witnessed (and admittedly have actively engaged in myself) is an increasing obsession with consumerism and populism. This is manifested by charismatic leaders who entrench their power base through telling the people (vegans) what they want to hear without being able to deliver on those claims or promises. We see this in the rhetoric of 'winning' promoted by celebri-vegans, when the statistics show a very different story. At times there is an almost cult-like refusal from some within the movement to examine, analyse and engage in constructive criticism as a means for progress. And if vegans who are animal advocates are unwilling to foster critical discussions, some of which may be personally uncomfortable, how will they know when they're getting it wrong? How will they be able to qualitatively assess the effects of their activism?

Social media has become the primary means by which animal rights activists convey their actions, investigations and messages into the broader community. A cursory scroll through Facebook throws up an extensive list of vegan activist pages, vegan cooking pages, animal rights and liberation pages, groups dedicated to listing other animals in shelters, pages for festivals, restaurants, clothing brands. Veganism and animal rights are more visible online than ever before. Commensurate to the proliferation of veganism and animal rights content across social media has come the adoption of activism as an individual identity in and of itself. This is evident by the pages set up for individual full-time activists relying upon the financial benefices of their followers to maintain both their activism and their lifestyles. Protest actions are engaged in openly and publicly and streamed live. The revolution will not be televised, it is currently being live-streamed directly to Facebook. It seems that efficacy is to be measured by the number of reactions, comments, views and share posts on social media received, not by the tangible outcomes achieved for other animals.

This approach, like any, has its positives and its pitfalls. When open rescue was conceptualised and first practiced in the early 90s in Australia, the philosophy centred around the transparency of intent and identity. It was about the normalising of rendering aid to other animals in need in a manner similar to how first responders render aid to humans. Photographs and film were taken when inside facilities and often disseminated to the broader public via the media (Open Rescue, 2020). Dissemination of footage and information was still heavily reliant upon a media outlet being willing to publish images and stories. Chat and blogging sites were available from the late 80s onwards but still restricted in their public reach. The influence of social media was yet to become widespread. Immediate gratification and global attention for activism was not yet a factor to be considered. The rise of Facebook has been rapid and it seems the vegan movement has not had time enough to adjust accordingly to its impact on its members and public interface.

In 2006 Facebook was opened for public use and by 2012 the social media site had amassed one billion online users. This gave corporations, organisations and individuals access to more online opportunities for connectivity than ever before. Today, there are 3.8 billion users of smartphones around the world (O'Dea, 2020). As a means to promote the message of veganism and animal liberation, the expansion of social media and the creation of the online activist identity seemed promising. Certainly it has helped in some regards with access to an audience being immediate and as expansive as your followers list (and theirs, if your content is deemed shareable). However, there is one fundamental aspect that vegans have failed to understand which has led to a muddying of the message, an inability to adapt, and even situations in which the safety of other animals has been jeopardised. And that is how social media has the ability to alter the processes of the human brain.

The brain produces an array of chemicals and hormones as it works to operate the human body. Dopamine acts as a chemical messenger between neurons and is released when the brain expects or receives a reward. It can be stimulated through food, sex, shopping, anything that is associated with feeling good. In anticipation of that something, the brain releases dopamine making the individual feel happy, or alert or motivated. The surge in dopamine upon receiving the reward then reinforces that anticipation and the positive feelings associated with its realisation in what is described as a "cycle of motivation, reward, and reinforcement" which is also known as a dopamine feedback loop (Haynes, 2018, n.p.). The brain also releases dopamine when the individual has successful social interactions with other people. This helps them establish relationships and the social groups upon which human survival is dependent. Haynes argues:

> Cognitive neuroscientists have shown that reward-ing social stimuli — laughing faces, positive recog-nition by our peers, messages from loved ones — activate the same dopaminergic reward pathways. Smartphones have provided us with a virtually unlimited supply of social stimuli, both positive and negative. Every notification, whether it's a text message, a 'like' on Instagram, or a Facebook notifi-cation, has the potential to be a positive social stim-ulus and dopamine influx. (2018, n.p)

As the individual is drawn further into the world of social media their chances of becoming addicted to the dopa-mine influx that occurs when they receive positive online interactions increases. Social media is constructed to cre-ate this addiction through dopamine driven feedback. The individual looks to their phone for a notification and the realisation of that notification creates a surge of dopamine which quickly subsides, encouraging them to look to their phone once again for that quick 'hit.' As Mahmudabad states:

> Clicks, likes, shares or retweets translate into little dopamine hits which inevitably, albeit unconsciously, push people towards holding views for which they will know they will receive appreciation. (2020, n.p.)

The individual swiftly learns that there are certain online opinions and identities that will receive greater amounts of positive feedback. They may, therefore, begin to craft these identities as their need for a 'hit' increases over time. The social media user effectively curates themselves for their followers and potential followers. What the individual says and how they say it is dependent upon what they think their followers would like them to say, for fear of losing likes or in the hopes of gaining more. Thus, whilst the individual may think they are generating persuasive content to contribute to important online dialogues, all too often they are being manufactured into content itself. Social media has had such a significant impact upon the way human brains and, as a result, society in general operates, that some former investors and executives involved in the creation of Facebook and social media have expressed their concerns and even regret at having facilitated its existence (Wong, 2017; Bilton, 2017; Garfield, 2017).

The implications this has for vegans' representations of activism online are significant but as yet have not been adequately explored, though online activism is often critiqued. The rapid transition from sporadic media attention (and dependence upon limited outlets such as self-printed zines) to quick-consume social media culture appears to have presented significant challenges. These challenges cannot have failed to have had an impact upon the activist community in the same way as it has literally changed how the internet-connected human society now operates. This may be seen in the rise of the celebri-vegan or influencer-activist, individuals whose entire online identity is carefully crafted so as to create the clout necessary to maintain a certain lifestyle, including global travel. For some activists who are involved in direct action, becoming absorbed into the social media matrix encourages an escalation of behaviour in order to maintain and increase the 'hits' received online. What begins with a sign outside of a slaughterhouse rapidly becomes a livestream from the operational slaughterhouse floor. This escalation is facilitated by the inevitable online appreciation for what you have done coupled with the perceived need to be 'doing the most.' Too often it can result in a lack consideration for self-critique and analysis that can prove problematic. Andrew X argues:

> Part of being revolutionary might be knowing when to stop and wait. It might be important to know how and when to strike for maximum effectiveness and also when to NOT strike. Activists have this "we must do something now!" attitude that seems fuelled by guilt. This is completely untactical. (2009, n.p.)

Delving further into the world of activism, then, it is suggested that many vegans and animal advocates may be driven by a desperate need to do something without thought to potential impacts or consequences. They can become ever more desperate to engage in actions of increasing intensity or to create an over-saturation of online content. Even when paired with the knowledge of the changes social media induce in brains, activists may nevertheless push themselves ever further onwards in pursuit of making a difference for other animals which can become entangled in the online high. This may have potentially serious consequences.

One such consequence is the muddying of the liberatory message of veganism through the creation of online identities that centre the individual activist. This can occur at the cost of a focus on the other animals. At its core, the liberation of other animals is a question of autonomy. It is about the fundamental right of other animals to exist free from the control and influence that is enforced by the human animal over all other species. Yet even in the act of facilitating the liberation of other animals there is possibly an element of control exerted by the activist. This control is a benign paternalism with the intent to remove the animal from a place of harm to a place of sanctuary. The activist action may not be experienced as freedom by the other animal.

Having engaged in aiding the liberation of other animals I now recognise that the individual animal will frequently display signs of fear, even a refusal to be removed from a cage or pen. This is due to that space being the only reference point with which they are familiar. The mere presence of a person, irrespective of their intent, can have the potential to cause stress. As such it becomes imperative not only to be mindful of one's actions within the space of the facility, but to also be mindful of how activists present that act of liberation and the language used to describe the act.

In one notable example, a well-known activist with a significant global following took a photo of themselves in front of animals being held in a slaughterhouse pen. The photo centred the activist in the foreground and showed the animals to be clearly scared of their presence as they recoiled as a group to the back of the pen. Yet the language used described the image to be the 'best selfie ever.' Regardless of the intent, the message this image and the language used to describe it undermined the fundamental principles of animal liberation. It denied the animals whatever little autonomy they had left to them in that space of exploitation and violence. To them, the activist was no different to their oppressors, in fact they belonged to the same group of beings responsible for the incarceration of the pigs and their eventual slaughter. That is not to say the plight of the animals should not have been documented as a means to expose the realities of animal exploitation. Documentation is a cornerstone of the movement without which animal advocates would not have the evidence necessary to undermine public confidence in these industries. However, placing one's self as the focal point of that documentation disregards the apparent discomfort of the documented animals. The subsequent use of profoundly inappropriate descriptive language for the image itself can have the effect of confirming that other animals are tools that can be utilised in pursuit of online content and interaction.

Language is powerful. A simple word can convey a wealth of nuances that may help (or hinder) the expression of ideas. Even as I write, Microsoft Word is advising me to change the word 'who' to 'that' as regards the lambs and the spiders. In my workshop at Vegan Festival Adelaide 2020 entitled *Re-centering animals: A focus on language* I deconstructed the use of the word 'voiceless' as a descriptive term for other animals. It is generally understood that animals are not voiceless per se, and the most common example used to prove this point is the screams of other animals as they are slaughtered. Their vocalisations en route to slaughter and during the process can be interpreted as indicators of their fear and their pain. However, for my workshop I chose to use another example, one that was less steeped in violence.

The cleaner wrasse is a small fish who lives on coral reefs throughout the oceans of the world. Their diet primarily consists of parasites and dead tissue cleaned from the skin of other larger marine animals including turtles, manta rays and even sharks. The relationship between these marine animals and the wrasse is mutualistic, providing the wrasse with a reliable source of food whilst providing considerable health benefits for the recipients of their cleaning services (Soares, 2017). When these visitors of varying species attend the cleaning stations both they and the wrasse must communicate with each other. The wrasse will perform a series of movements and posturing and the 'clients' as they are referred to, having recognised the lateral stripe running the length of the wrasse's body and the meaning of their body languge, will adopt a posture themselves to indicate their peaceful intent and desire to be cleaned (Stummer, Weller, Johnson & Coté, 2005). Throughout the cleaning, the wrasse will maintain constant contact with their client using their pelvic fins which encourages them to remain in place (Bshary, 2003). This is truly remarkable, for the wrasse is able to interpret the body language of multiple different species and communicate back to them, all of whom communicate in species-specific ways. In this regard, the cleaner wrasse may in fact be considered multilingual. Indeed, this mutualistic relationship has been stated to be crucial not just for the individual health of the wrasse and of their clients but for the overall health of the reefs which these fish inhabit (Bshary, 2003). They are multilingual, communicative, co-operative and mutualistic. But there is one thing the cleaner wrasse cannot be called, nor indeed the many other marine animals who utilise their cleaning services, and that is voiceless.

By describing other animals as voiceless, humans effectively exclude them from their own movement and position humans as 'the voices.' This othering of animals is unfortunately a consequence in a movement dominated by human voices and human personalities. Even the use of 'other' or 'non-human' to describe animals sets humans apart from them. They are other and human is the default position (Braidotti, 2013). At the same time to say human and animal likewise creates a delineation between humans and other animals that denies humans very animality. Humans seemingly have an obsession with their own uniqueness within the context of the natural world (Mason, 2005). This is not the individual's fault per se, rather, it is an attitude they are raised into, whether it be through the feeding of flesh to them as children, the information they receive during their education, or the attitudes of peers. Mason states:

> The idea of human uniqueness makes no sense scientifically, for it is not something that exists in the real living world. For these reasons alone, it should be rejected, for it gives us a false basis for our place in the world. If we want to come to terms with nature, we must be honest about the realities of nature and honest about ourselves as real animals in it. True, we have unique abilities, but so does every other animal. (2005, p. 281)

Certainly the cleaner wrasse could not write a symphony but nor do we possess the language skills of the cleaner wrasse that enables them to safely clean inside the mouths of sharks. Speciesism may not be an attitude of the individual's own making but each person can perpetuate discrimination against other animals or change towards pro-animal equality. Human exceptionalism and supremacy must be deconstructed (Braidotti, 2018) as part of the reimagining of the social spaces in which humans and non-humans alike are all held. This becomes possible when humans reconnect with our own inherent animality and the natural world to which they belong. Haraway argues:

> No species, not even our own arrogant one pretending
> to be good individuals in so-called modern Western
> scripts, acts alone; assemblages of organic species and
> of abiotic actors make history, the evolutionary kind
> and the other kinds too. (2015, p. 159)

Why do humans as an animal species have this obsession
with uniqueness? For current purposes, it is troubling to
consider the extent to which animal advocates and activists might adopt language that contributes to the othering
of animals and excludes them from their own movement.
The human inhabitants of the Global North were raised in
societies built upon industrial agriculture (and the enforced
establishment of industrial agriculture in the Global South).
This has created a dominant worldview that is contemptuous
of other animals where societal views, actions and language
have evolved as a means to maintain a position of dominion
over the natural world (Mason, 2005). Mason explains that
this is achieved by creating and maintaining a hierarchy:

> A stewardship model is paternalistic, and still presumes
> a ladder of being with humans running the world in a
> kind of benevolent dictatorship. Stewardship, many
> believe, is simply a euphemism for dominionism; it
> is old wine in new bottles. Its hierarchical nature can
> be demonstrated by applying the model to human
> relations. (2005, p. 282)

It is important to note that the idea of stewardship as
described by Mason (2005) is different from Australian

Aboriginal peoples' commitment to stewardship of their lands as a deep respectful and mutual caring for other living beings (Poelina, 2020). Other animals may be liberated from their cages but beyond this they are still under the control of humans who will determine the best places and conditions for them to live in. Again, I am not suggesting leaving animals who have been domesticated by humans to fend for themselves in the wild or the streets. The indiscriminate breeding of other animals has resulted in mammals in the natural world accounting for only 4% of the Earth's mammalian biomass. Humans cannot and indeed should not abrogate the responsibility to provide sanctuary for the dispossessed and the exploited (Bar-On, Phillips, & Milo, 2018).

Nevertheless the language used to describe the human-animal relationship is crucial to interrogate as part of unpacking the species hierarchy. This hierarchy between species is one where the "balance of power is that the human is always dominant" (Burke & Iannuzzi cited in Peggs, 2017, p. 103). Speciesist language such as voiceless holds other animals in such contempt as to deprive them of their autonomy even when it is believed to be acting in their best interests. The chicken will herald the laying of an egg with raucous crowing and the rabbit will express their amorous intent with loving grunts. A dog may whimper in fear of fireworks and the humpback whale fills the oceans with languages that humans have only just begun to translate. To call them voiceless is not only inaccurate, it denies them the full expression of agency that is rightfully theirs. As Roy explains "we know of course there is no such thing as the 'voiceless.' There are only the deliberately silenced, or the preferably unheard" (2004, n.p.). As celebri-veganism gains momentum through social media in its relentless pursuit of mainstream popularity there is a growing divide between those who claim to speak for the animals and those who wish to facilitate other animals to speak for themselves. The vegan movement is at a stage where the cult of personality is taking over the drive for other animals' liberation.

The cult of personality is typically a political tactic that utilises mass (social) media, spectacle and propaganda as a means to cultivate an idealised image of a leader, often through unquestioning public flattery in support of the leader/s of the state (Pisch, 2016). Similar tactics are observable in the use of social media as a marketing tool to create an online identity that uses the spectacle of activism to attract positive online affirmation. Sometimes this can also include the pursuit of financial gain such as the creation of accounts on Patreon or being in receipt of direct funding by larger mainstream organisations. In late 2020 it was revealed that an anonymous benefactor has been donating millions of dollars every year to a handful of high profile individuals and groups. This led to numerous people raising concerns over financial misappropriation and the ethics of large-scale capitalist investment in social justice movements. Best argues:

> Indeed, mainstream organizations are themselves
> capitalist bureaucracies that accumulate coveted
> money and influence from the corporate-state system,

and thus, are hardly subversive institutions breeding
the next generation of radicals. (2014, p. 85)

The distribution (or maldistribution) of funds and
resources to elite groups that operate under hierarchical
systems in the animal industrial complex is positioning the
mainstream vegan movement as just another brick in the
capitalist wall. It is further compounded by the elite groups
depending upon the labour of unknown and unpaid volunteers who create product for consumption (events, online
content, merchandise) in pursuit of brand power. All the
black hoodies and brooding selfies in the world cannot make
these systems of dominance revolutionary.

This is not isolated to the animal rights movement by
any means as the concept of creating an online identity and
marketing that identity in pursuit of some form of income
is the very basis of social media influencer culture. However,
the elevation of certain individuals (or indeed groups) as
leaders within a political movement such as the animal
liberation movement and the cultivation of those identities
through social media marketing all too often leads to a lack
of accountability. Criticisms relating to use of language and
imagery or the efficacy of certain actions are perceived (or
deliberately misrepresented) as an attack on the movement
itself as a means to deflect negative attention. Yet criticism
is a necessary tool for progress, as pattrice jones (she does
not capitalise her name) states:

Every activist and organisation ought to be able to identify the assumptions about people and how the world works that underlie their strategies and tactics and be willing to revise those theories in response to new information. Activism is always a process of trial and error, and only reflection can allow us to see when we need to tweak our tactics or even change course altogether. (cited in Forest, 2020, n.p.)

Critics, no matter how diplomatic, are at best labelled divisive or at worst are 'bad-jacketed' with unfounded accusations of being police or agent provocateurs levelled at any who dare criticise the leaders. This can result in their ostracism from the movement. The cult of personality may stymie the very discussions needed to qualitatively assess the efficacy or potentially detrimental facts of animal advocates' activism, thus preventing the movement from progressing.

This lack of accountability and a reliance upon social media (with its associated manipulation of the very functioning of individuals' brains) can have disastrous consequences for other animals, not simply in the assessment of efficacy but in the more immediate term. It can lead to a complete disregard for an online security culture resulting in other animals whose liberations have been facilitated being seized by the state and returned to the sites of their former incarceration. For a majority of these animals this means a death sentence, as bio control measures mean they cannot be reintroduced back into the food system, or they may have aged out of the slaughter age bracket whilst in sanctuary. Where other animals have been liberated from facilities their safety must be held as paramount. Their locations must remain hidden. No messages indicating their whereabouts should be retained, all photographs should have their EXIF data removed and no photographs should be taken that identify the location. In 2017 the FBI initiated a multistate hunt for two piglets liberated from a Smithfield-owned piggery in Utah. Two farmed animal sanctuaries in Utah and Colorado were raided with other pigs living there mutilated by FBI agents as a means to collect DNA samples (Meek, 2019). The FBI agents were prepared to mutilate piglets unrelated to those whose liberation had been facilitated in order to intimidate and hopefully charge activists under the Animal Enterprise Terrorism Act (Greenwald, 2017). Had the piglets been found they would have been killed. This is the extent to which the authorities will go in pursuit of liberated animals as a means to curtail activists. Animals reclaimed by the industries they were liberated from are mere tools in pursuit of political dissidents. As such, activists must be sure to maintain a culture of security around the whereabouts of these animals because their safety is paramount.

Perhaps the issue is not whether activism is public or private. Perhaps the issue is instead with the isolationist position that the adoption of an activist identity itself can create. Activism, especially public activism, necessitates that one person or a group of persons act where a majority of others may not be able or willing, creating an inequitable division of labour and often resources. Andrew X explains:

A division of labour implies that one person takes on a role on behalf of many others who relinquish this responsibility. A separation of tasks means that other people will grow your food and make your clothes and supply your electricity while you get on with achieving social change. The activist, being an expert in social change, assumes other people aren't doing anything to change their lives and so feels a duty or a responsibility to do it on their behalf. Activists think they are compensating for the lack of activity by others. Defining ourselves as activists means defining our actions as the ones which will bring about social change, thus disregarding the activity of thousands of other non-activists. (2009, n.p)

Within the world of animal advocacy, the division of labour is obscured by a dependency on social media as an effective means of communication and the rise of influencer-culture. Patreon and other sources of crowdfunding have been seized upon by some who cultivate an online identity as an activist through content creation, attending festivals, protests, vigils and actions without actively assisting in the funding or organising of those events. This behaviour is simultaneously praised by followers and denigrated by others as saviourism. Amongst follower circles, it is deemed acceptable that others will work jobs to obtain income and then reimburse the full-time activist for their content creation or attendance at events. Further, it is accepted that others will pay for food, amenities, travel and housing whilst being told they (or rather the animals, who are conveniently denied agency) need the activist to exist on their behalf. The centering of the celebri-vegans as the appointed representatives of other animals overlooks not only the agency of other animals themselves, but also exploits the work done by the anonymous investigators, organisers and volunteers. Most of the work is done by activists who also work part-time or full-time jobs outside of animal advocacy. Their activist volunteerism is used to support the full-time activist's platform and lifestyle.

While there is a degree of social elevation that can be crafted through the promoted role of the activist, there is also a degree of social isolation that results from engagement within advocacy. For myself personally, my job prospects have been increasingly impacted the more public my actions or commentary has become. Sometimes activists actively cultivate that isolation, potentially to the detriment of their efficacy within the broader community. For example, the Liberation Pledge encourages vegans and activists to refuse to sit at table with anyone consuming products taken from the bodies of other animals. This is entirely understandable and a person cannot be faulted for wishing to remove themselves from exposure to that which is representative of industrialised violence and horror against other animals. Certainly one would not expect anti-racists to associate with those who promote racist ideology and there is no reason why sitting at a table with individuals engaging in acts of violence against other animals should be regarded any differently. But it also necessitates a withdrawal from the company of family, friends and communities. As such it can instead lead to a reduction of the social interactions required to promote the concept of animal liberation within our own circles. Isolationism may also result in a reliance upon activist circles for our social groups which can create toxic interdependencies and echo chambers from which it may be difficult to extricate one's self. The closed system this can cause is compounded if that social group adheres to a hierarchical structure at the top of which is situated one or several charismatic leaders who have amassed followings online and in person. Isolation from the broader community and reliance upon a set group of individuals for social and activist engagement has the potential to undermine the reach of the message and instead create echo chambers. In such circumstances animal advocates may perceive themselves to be affecting great change when in fact they are confined to a web-like system of hierarchies and domination that restricts their movement and contribution within the broader community.

There is evidence that the mainstream approach that combines activist identity with online celebrity as well as the active promotion of an apolitical go vegan message is simply not effective. Certainly there is more visibility for veganism and animal rights but according to data collected via polls it seems that this visibility is not resulting in a mass adoption of veganism or even of plant-based diets. A 2010 Eat Well poll of 1262 participants indicated that roughly 1% of Australians identified as vegans. In 2019 the ABC's *Australia talks national survey* of 25 788 people revealed that same number (Australia Eat Well, 2010; Sutton, 2019). An Institut de Publique Sondage d'Opinion Secteur (IPSOS) investigation into diets around the world indicated roughly 3% of the global population identified as vegan (IPSOS, 2020). The fastest growing vegan demographic is Black Americans, with 8% now reportedly living vegan (Reiley, 2020). But for the most part, global consumption of animal products is increasing and shows no signs of stopping. The animal industrial complex is as strong as ever, irrespective of the numbers of vegans, prevalence of online activity, or the numbers of protest actions held in recent years.

But perhaps one of the most problematic issues with mainstream animal rights activism is the creation of a phenomenon I will refer to as the 'activist industrial complex.' This idea refers to a system of myriad connections between corporatised activism organisations that are dependent upon an extensive volunteer labour base to sell the brand along with 'the message.' The activist industrial complex operates as an extension of the charitable industrial complex which Spade defines in the following way:

> Charity is increasingly privatized and contracted out to the massive nonprofit sector. Nonprofits compete for grants to address social problems. Elite donors get to decide what strategies should be funded and then protect their money from taxation by storing it in foundations that fund their pet projects [...]. Nonprofitization has reproduced antidemocratic

racist and colonial relationships between the winners and losers of extractive, exploitative economic arrangements. (2020, p. 140)

In the traditional structure of the industrial complex the nexus between government and corporations is positive with the government working to create market environments conducive to corporate advancement. But, as discussed in the first essay, government often actively works in opposition to the grassroots activist community, through attempts to inhibit the expression of protest or dissent. Siriniwasa (2020) refers to the activist industrial complex in terms of the networks of non-government organisations, activist groups and community organisations that connect with federal, state and local government. My definition of the activist industrial complex differs in that it acts as a microcosm within the macrocosm of industrial complexes where a small number of perceived elites take on the responsibility of governance within the movement, creating both consumer and labour resource markets. Consumer resource markets consist of those individuals who view and engage with online content, purchase branded merchandise, or donate money to the organisation (or individual influencer activists). Labour resource markets comprise of those volunteers who are often targeted by the selected individuals chosen to engage in activism tours designed to create new chapters or to instruct new activists according to the predetermined blueprints of that group. Both Siriniwasa (2020) and myself agree that prestige within the activist industrial complex is derived from social media influencer culture.

How does the activist industrial complex manifest within communities? An example is the denigration of those who do not engage in activism by those who do, the questions 'well what are you doing?' There is a risk of falling into the trap of negatively judging those who are doing 'less' than those who are 'doing the most.' It can take focus and energy from the liberation effort and be divisive and corrosive within the activist group and their communities. The entire activist identity can become framed by this often guilt-driven need to do something, anything at all. And so they 'do.' Then they post about their actions online for the distribution to and approbation of their peers; and they're not allowed to stop, either spurred on by the encouragement of their activist peers or by the increasingly ingrained sense of guilt and desperation. If not them, then who after all.

This dynamic represents a strategic manipulation designed to push individuals further, to produce more activism, more content, more labour under the brand banner of the organisation or movement. As activism becomes dominated by these corporate organisations that enforce a hierarchy upon those working under their brand whilst accepting the largesse of capitalist investors, a reliance on a repetitive activism structure becomes evident. There is little variation in activism from the mainstream focus on street outreach or bearing witness at facilities. Through these actions the activist can become traumatised and then re-traumatised with the implicit expectation that the individual's trauma must be broadcast on social media 'for the animals.' This can manifest as tear-stained selfies, long posts detailing the violence and the horrors seen. There is very little consideration for the psychological harms caused to activists who share their experiences or to the audience. There is a constant pursuit of funding with donation drives online that involve spamming live stream comment sections with links or the sale of merchandise that is routinely re-branded. The re-branding occurs despite significant issues with fast fashion and over-consumption irrespective of how ethical the manufacturing process is claimed to be. In this and other ways, the corporate activist organisations have effectively developed brand power and pursued financial gain via the labour of mostly unseen and unpaid individuals. Individuals' experiences of trauma are effectively commodified under a system that demands more of them, subsumes them into the complex as units of production, then burns them out.

In some high profile cases (and many that have remained concealed) that trauma has not been caused purely by exposing the individual to horrific acts of violence against other animals, or to the apathetic response of the broader community. Rather it has been caused by another member of the activist community through harassment, bigotry and sexual predation. I will not include specific cases here as the traumas of these individuals are not mine to broadcast. Suffice to say there have been several high profile cases in recent years in which the individuals who have come forward with their stories have been subjected to an onslaught of online vitriol for daring to speak out. Corporate activist organisations may have human resources representatives whose task it is to address complaints of this nature (a reflection of structures within the broader corporate world). However they have proven woefully inadequate at addressing the claims that have been made, and of offering assistance to the aggrieved person/s, or indeed in mitigating the vicious onslaught those aggrieved individuals have all too often received. This is not to be wondered at when activists have modelled their organisations upon prevailing corporate structures. It is perhaps inevitable that the prevailing social attitudes towards dissent and complaints will inform the implemented structures. Spade explains that "systems of domination produce routes for channelling dissatisfaction that are non-threatening to those systems. We are encouraged to bring our complaints in ways that are the most beneficial to existing conditions" (2020, p. 134).

Hierarchies and competing brands within activism utilise the framework of dominant social structures. Just as many have experienced in the corporate world, it seems to be easier to sweep allegations under the carpet rather than addressing the issues involved including the culture that gives abusive individuals access to potential vulnerable members of the activist community. Adopting corporate structure as a model for organisations ostensibly pursuing the goals of social justice can only prove an obstruction to the reimagining of the social spaces. This is contributing to significant numbers of activists leaving the community due to burn out, incidents that occur within the community and the commodification of their trauma. All too often the burned out activists find themselves ostracised and bereft of the social support networks they formerly found within the activist groups into which they had been entirely subsumed. Meanwhile, the corporate activist organisations continue to elevate select personalities to go on missionary-esque global tours in order to create new chapters and new activists. The creation of paid positions funded largely by donations or sales entrench the culture of hierarchy and celebri-vegans. Too often the on-the-ground activist and their trauma has become a commodity to be used up and spat out in pursuit of clout and cash.

One cannot help but consider the words of Top Dollar from the 1994 cult classic *The Crow*: "A [hu]man has an idea. The idea attracts others, likeminded. The idea expands, the idea becomes the institution. What was the idea?" (Proyas, 1994, n.p.). We had an idea once, the liberation of other animals from the yoke of human exploitation. As the idea has expanded, and as corporate influence has infiltrated the activist community and mainstream expressions of activism have proliferated, the idea has become entrapped in an industrial complex. The idea has become the institution consuming individuals on a vast scale. Top Dollar also exhorted his followers to "set a fire so goddamn big, the gods will notice us again" (Proyas, 1994, n.p.). This certainly has been a tactic that is part of an alternative approach utilised over the years by some individuals operating under the banner of the ALF. This is a decentralised anonymous collective whose identities remain mostly concealed (unless an individual is arrested) yet are held in high regard by most within the vegan and animal liberation movements. Whilst I am not encouraging the reader to engage in arson as a tactic, the ALF does represent a movement that has successfully disrupted, and in some cases, destroyed animal exploitation facilities and industries. They have done this without the need for corporate branding, hierarchy or a dependency upon the cult of personality to pursue their ends. It is possible to resist the harmful aspects of the activist industrial complex and at the same time to challenge and undermine the animal industrial complex.

Is activism over? I'm not sure. Certainly the pandemic and associated social disruptions have shut down the more mainstream expressions of activism, such as vigils or street outreach as well as activism tours. Perhaps that's why we're seeing such a ruckus currently. The influencer activists who have relied upon those forms of activism to create their platforms for so long are struggling to remain relevant. Many do not have the ability or desire to diversify their activism and simultaneously maintain their status. As the pandemic continues, diversification and accessibility of activism is more necessary than ever before, as the impacts are felt not only by human communities but other animal communities. In November 2020 Danish authorities announced a plan to kill up to 17 million mink held captive in fur production facilities, due to the spread of a mutated strain of coronavirus transmissible between mink and humans (Murray, 2020). The announcement was heralded by global outcry by vegans, animal advocates and the general community, but commenced nonetheless. The mass killing was also opposed by the mink farmers themselves who believe it could spell the end of the mink fur industry in Denmark just as the coronavirus destroyed the industry in the Netherlands, a grim silver lining (Murray, 2020). Since the announcement of the cull over 10 million mink have been slaughtered, requiring hasty mass burials that in some areas have resulted in the corpses of slain animals rising from their graves due to the accumulated gases from decomposition (Hart, 2020). This case though horrific to comprehend does present a unique opportunity to campaign for the end of the fur industry. Evidently there is still a need for activism.

What I am sure of is that now is the time for the activist identity to die. The isolationist attitudes, the hoarding of knowledge, resources and opportunity, the hierarchies and the fame game must end. It's time to let go of the hierarchical structures and corporatisation of activism and instead pursue justice on a genuinely grassroots level via nonviolent means that reach into the broader community. This can only be achieved if we recognise activism as praxis, as the practical application of that which we learn through experience or through theory, and not as an identity or brand. Because if there is one thing that is abundantly clear it is that what other animal activists are currently doing is not working. As the essays have shown, the numbers of animals slaughtered continue to increase and the continued growth of the animal industrial complex obstructs the pursuit of justice for other animals. These exploitative systems cannot be reformed to become more suitable to other animal liberation goals, they must be replaced or entirely destroyed. By shedding systems and models that are counter-intuitive to the actualisation of liberation we free ourselves to move more effectively towards a future that is inclusive of all. I'll see you all in the streets!

References

Andrew X (2009). *Give up activism*. https://www.theanarchistlibrary.org/library/andrew-x-give-up-activism

Australian Eat Well (2014). *Vegetarianism in Australia*. https://www.australianeatwell.com. au/facts-and-figures/vegetarianism-in-australia

Bar-On, Y. M., Phillips, R., & Milo, R. (2018). The biomass distribution on Earth. *Proceedings of the National Academy of Sciences of the United States of America, 115*(25), 6506-6511. https://doi.org/10.1073/pnas.1711842155

Best, S. (2014). *The politics of total liberation: Revolution for the 21st century*. Palgrave Macmillan.

Bilton, N. (2017). *'Oh my god, what have I done': Some early Facebook employees regret the monster they created*. https://www.vanityfair.com/news/2017/10/early-facebook-employees-regret-the-monster-they-created

Braidotti, R. (2013). *The posthuman*. Polity Press.

Braidotti, R. (2018). A theoretical framework for the critical posthumanities. *Theory, Culture and Society, 0*(0), 1-31.

Bshary, R. (2003). The cleaner wrasse, labroides dimidiatus, is a key organism for reef fish diversity at Ras Mohammad National Park, Egypt. *Journal of Animal Ecology, 72*(1), 169-72. https://doi.org/10.1046/j.1365-2656.2003.00683.x

Forest, D. (2020). *Intersectional animal advocacy: An interview with*

pattrice jones. https://www.animalpeopleforum.org/2020/08/26/
intersectional-animal-advocacy-an-interview-with-pattrice-
jones/

Garfield, L. (2017). *These tech execs have regrets about the
world-changing sites they helped create.* https://businessinsider.
com/social-media-affects-society-tech-execs-2017-12

Greenwald, G. (2017). *The FBIs hunt for two missing piglets reveals
the federal coverup of barbaric factory farms.* https://www.
theintercept.com/2017/10/05/factory-farms-fbi-missing-
piglets-animal-rights-glenn-greenwald

Haraway, D. (2015). Anthropocene, Capitalocene, Planationocene,
Chthulucene: Making kin. *Environmental Humanities, 6,* 159-165.

Hart, R. (2020). *Denmark wants to exhume 'zombie mink' rising
from mass graves while scientists warn of permanent covid-19
pandemicrisk.*https://www.forbes.com/sites/roberthart/2020/11/27/
denmark-wants-to-exhume-zombie-mink-from-mass-graves-
while-scientists-warn-of-permanent-covid-19-pandemic-risk/
amp/

Haynes, T. (2018). *Dopamine, smartphones & you: A battle for
your time.* https://sitn.hms. harvard.edu/flash/2018/dopamine-
smartphones-battle-time/

Institut de Publique Sondage d'Opinion Secteur, IPSOS (2018).
Diets around the world: An exploration. https://www.ipsos.
com/en/diets-around-the-world-exploration

Mahmudabad, A. (2020). *Social media and populist politicians
are natural bedfellows.* https://www.thewire.in/tech/social-

media-populist-politicians-facebook-bjp-hate-speech

Mason, J. (2005). *An unnatural order: The roots of our destruction of nature*. Lantern Books.

Meek, T. (2019). *Smithfield Foods: How many pigs does Smithfield slaughter per day?* https://www.sentientmedia.org/smithfield-foods/

Murray, A. (2020). *Coronavirus: Denmark shaken by cull of millions of mink*. https://www.bbc. com/news/world-europe-54890229

O'Dea, S. (2020). *Smartphone users worldwide 2016-2021*. https://www.statista.com/statistics/330695/number-of-smartphone-users-worldwide/

Open Rescue (2020). *About open rescue*. https://www.openrescue.org/about/index.htm

Peggs, K. (2017). What have animals to do with social work? A sociological reflection on species and social work. *Journal of Animal Ethics, 7*(1), 96-108.

Pisch, A. (2016). *The personality cult of Stalin in Soviet posters 1929-1953: Archetypes, inventions and fabrications*. ANU Press.

Poelina, A. (2020). Foreword. First Law is the natural law of the land. In D. Ross, M. Brueckner, M. Palmer & W. Eaglehawk (Eds.), *Eco-activism & social work: New directions in leadership and group work* (pp. viii-xii). Routledge.

Proyas, A. (1994). *The Crow*. Dimension Films.

Reiley, L. (2020). *The fastest-growing vegan demographic is*

African Americans. https://www.washingtonpost.com/
business/2020/01/24/fastest-growing-vegan-Demographic-
is-african-americans-wu-tang-clan-other-hip-hop-
acts-paved-way

Roy, A. (2004). *Peace and the new corporate liberation theology:
2004 Sydney Peace Prize lecture.* https://www.sydney.edu.au/
news/84.html?newsstoryvid=279

Siriniwasa, H. (2020). *Allyship, safety and the activist-industrial-
complex.* https://honisoit.com/2020/09/allyship-safety-and-
the-activist-industrial-complex/

Soares, M. (2017). The neurobiology of mutualistic behavior: The
cleanerfish swims into the spotlight. *Frontiers in Behavioural
Neuroscience, 11*(191), 1-12. doi: 10.3389/fnbeh.2017.00191

Spade, D. (2020). Solidarity not charity: Mutual aid for mobilisation
and survival. *Social Text, 142, 38*(1), 131-151.

Stummer, L., Weller, J., Johnson, M., & Coté, I. (2005). Size and
stripes: How clients recognise cleaners. *Animal Behaviour, 68*(1),
145-150.

Sutton, M. (2019). *Vegans a 1 per cent minority in a country of meat
eaters, survey finds.* https://www.abc.net.au/news/2019-10-26/
vegans-comprise-just-1-per-cent-of-the-population-survey-
finds/116353306

Wong, J. (2017). *Former Facebook executive: Social media is
ripping society apart.* https://www.theguardian.com/
technology/2017/dc/11/facebook-former-executive-ripping-
society-apart

CONCLUSION
I'm not scared of spiders anymore

"These laws of yours are no different from spider's webs. They'll restrain anyone weak and insignificant who gets caught in them, but they'll be torn to shreds by people with power and money."
— *Anacharsis (Plutarch, c. 100ce/1998)*

Many humans have a profound fear of spiders. I myself am working towards letting go of an arachnophobia that has no justification in reality. In truth, the more I seek to understand spiders, the more respect and consideration I have for them. There are several I now share my home with, and though their webs may be causing a few issues as they turn my light fittings into living larders, I am finding co-existence to be mostly equanimous. Whilst there is still an instinctual fear there is also understanding.

I have used the metaphor of the spider's web extensively throughout this work as an analogy for the interconnected systems of government, institutions and corporations that influence and control individuals' lived experiences in an increasingly industrialised and digitalised world. My use of this analogy unfortunately places spiders on the same level as wealthy politicians, CEOs and capitalists, tapping into that primal fear of the predatory web maker. But this could not be further from the truth. Spiders create webs and hunt within precariously balanced ecosystems fulfilling a function that is critical for those systems and eating only for their survival. The creators and beneficiaries of the animal industrial complex destroy ecosystems (Higgins, 2010) and are not predatory on others out of necessity but from the desire to maximise profits at the expense of all other life on Earth (Moore, 2016). Spiders are a necessity; billionaires less so.

The problem is that as a society humans have become so ensnared in this way of life, that many people can see no way clear. Exploitation, suffering, slaughter and ecocide have become normalised to the extent that they are now naturalised. Humans cling to those threads, the hierarchies and modes of manufacture and control, even as they strangle many of us, fracture our communities, manipulate our brains, and drag us ever closer to our demise as a species interrelatedly with other animals (Intergovernmental Science-Policy Platform on Biodiversity and Ecosystem Services, 2019). The spider's web is an ephemeral thing and its beauty lies in its very fragility. The picture I have painted throughout this work is neither beautiful nor ephemeral. Instead it is a grim representation of the current state of affairs. It is important to recognise that the web of politics, industry and their control over society is nonetheless fragile. Care must be taken in our acknowledgement of its existence not to overstate its strength. As Twine states:

> It is worth pointing to a note of caution toward the discourse of the complex in the sense that it may suggest something akin to a conspiracy theory. On the one hand it points to relatively powerful alliances and networks in particular sectors of the global economy that strive to maintain a hegemonic position. It underlines how capital accumulation and resource control may become the overriding rationale in spheres such as global food production or military conflict and how these relations are implicated and used as conduits for geopolitical strategies. Yet it would be a mistake arguably to overplay the degree of control that particular actors and actor-networks are assumed to have. In other words the discourse of the complex ought not to become fatalistic. (2012, p. 20)

The web of the animal industrial complex has weaknesses, the threads can be disrupted and they can be pulled. Further, animal liberation work necessitates a combination of tactics and strategies that look beyond apolitical veganism and the social segregation (or indeed corporate exploitation) of the activist. Collaborations between unlikely allies and collective actions are needed that seek to disrupt supply chains and financial systems. It is not enough to rely upon vague notions of 'planting seeds' or 'changing hearts and minds.' Yes, the influence of government and corporations are seemingly overwhelming and the task of deconstructing those systems is daunting. But it can be done. The key is to develop our own power as communities and to apply a wealth of knowledge and strategy to the task of deconstructing the web.

Perhaps the answer is to let the animals lead in their resistance and for humans to listen to them. This may seem an unreasonable notion under the circumstances presented by human domination of the world and the spaces which other animals inhabit. The oppressor is unlikely to allow the escape of those they oppress, not least of all when there are profits to be made. Then there is the question of cognition, whether other animals understand they are oppressed and therefore are able to effectively resist their oppression. Certainly they are more than aware of imminent danger when they are waiting in slaughterhouses or places of similar violence. As Allen and Essen state:

> Animal resistors might well feel threatened, sense that their lives are at risk, and that running away from the humans in their present relational field will reduce this threat. Moreover, they might well *intend* to reduce this risk by running away. In other words, running away might well be an intentional act based on a perception of danger rather than a merely arbitrary or random act – 'just running away.' (2018, p. 14)

With this understanding it seems other animals are capable of resistance in reaction to a threatening situation. I have personally witnessed this on the kill floor at the Luv-a-Duck slaughterhouse in 2018. The deafening sounds of machinery and other ducks vocalising and the cloying smell of blood and excrement in the air make it very apparent that this is a place of violence. It is a stimulus that the thousands of ducks kept crated awaiting their inevitable slaughter are certainly aware of. Many of the highest stacked crates were without tops, but the ducks did not fly out being under-developed seven-week old babies as they were, and seeking protection within the familiarity of their flock. For some reason two ducks did choose to jump from the crates to the floor. Perhaps they had seen activists removing a number of ducks from other crates, perhaps they smelt the fresh water in the paddling pools we had filled. Whatever it was that drove this lonely pair to leave the crates, they then permitted themselves to be collected by activists who then ran them to safety in what Allen and Essen would describe as an act of "interspecies co-liberation" (2018, p. 4).

Reactive resistance by other animals is certainly well documented. From cows escaping slaughterhouses, to bulls charging down matadors or leaping into the stands crowded with spectators and pigs leaping from the top levels of moving slaughter trucks. The desire of other animals seeking to avoid harm and acting as agents of their own resistance is apparent. In 2020 the Farm Transparency Project (FTP) released covert footage from the Kankool Pet Meats slaughterhouse in New South Wales (FTP, 2020). A single cow saw an opportunity to escape the kill floor through the loading chute as the gate had become obstructed by a horse also awaiting slaughter. She ran, in a defiant act of resistance against those who would take her life. Sadly her escape was obstructed by a fence and she was shot before being carted back into the slaughterhouse where she was butchered. Nevertheless, her reaction to the threat of violence she sensed in that place was an expression of agency even if that agency was realised for only a moment in time.

But what of proactive resistance? In 2020 a series of attacks against yachts and fishing boats were orchestrated in waters from the Strait of Gibraltar to Galicia, in which vessels were damaged and crew members were injured (Ankel, 2020). It was not human pirates attacking the vessels rather groups of orcas had commenced aggressions against these boats for reasons that remain yet to be determined. One pod of orcas in particular appeared to be pursuing and attacking the boats, exhibiting behaviour that scientists described as highly unusual. Victoria Morris was aboard one of the yachts that came under attack in July. She described the incident to The Guardian thus:

> The noise was really scary. They were ramming the keel, there was this horrible echo, I thought they could capsize the boat. And this deafening noise as they communicated, whistling to each other. It was so loud we had to shout. (Smillie, 2020, n.p.)

The orcas communicated with each other. They spoke to one another with vocalisations whilst working together as a coordinated group to attack the vessel. The reasons for this behaviour are still unknown. Whilst boat strikes involving cetaceans are not uncommon as waterways become increasingly populated by humans and our machines, it is extremely rare for whales to deliberately ram boats without provocation (such as was documented during the long-boat whaling era). Many people commented it could be that the orcas associate the boats with fish and are seeking food, others that the orcas are seeking to remove the boats to protect their own food source. Rocío Espada, who works with the marine biology laboratory at the University of Seville, hypothesised that the deliberate ramming of boats with such force indicates the orcas are under stress, potentially as a result of calves previously becoming entangled in nets and long lines (Smillie, 2020). If this is the case, could the memory of calves killed by human fishing practices be driving the orcas to remove a remembered threat, or to exact revenge? Perhaps humans should avoid making such assumptions, the orcas reasons are after all their own. However, at the very least these attacks are producing "causal effects, setting in motion processes that change a system of institutionally mediated relations between animals and humans" (Allen & Essen, 2018, p. 25). As such their actions are in fact *direct actions* for other animal liberation.

When humans begin to view other animals through this lens, as being able to engage in both reactive and proactive acts of resistance, humans' own roles as animal advocates begin to shift. Thus, humans are not the saviours of other animals. Rather humans become co-liberators in the facilitation of other animals' own resistance. In fact humans can move beyond merely re-centering other animals within their own movement. Humans can instead place them directly at the helm, thus removing humans as the central focus of a liberatory movement. Human labours become the work of translators, facilitators, allies and accomplices as they strive to deconstruct the systems of misothery into which most of them were born and through which most of them were raised, systems that continue to inform their lives even as vegans or as activists. As subversive energy states:

> We should be attempting to create new ways of relating with the world that do not require 'enlightened' humans speaking on behalf of anyone, animals included. (2012, n.p.)

This is the direction I believe animal advocates must move towards, a truly revolutionary political ideal through which we could begin to create the socio-political systems that acknowledge each of us as having equal moral value, not in spite of our differences, but in recognition of them.

The core of revolution is not the pursuit of perfection. It is at the precise moment we demand that processes are commenced to begin the work of deconstructing oppressive regimes and systems that a revolution becomes a potential reality. A revolution is more than an idea. It is a process of evolution that seeks to take us beyond that which we know towards the achievement of the inalienable rights we all deserve. But progress can be painful and more often than not necessitates deeply uncomfortable experiences and conversations. I hope to have facilitated some of those conversations with my work. Certainly writing this treatise has been an evolution of ideas for me, where I have come to realise some painful truths relating to my own engagement within activism and the animal advocate community.

Finally, I find myself no longer afraid of spiders. Additionally, I am no longer afraid of the webs created by the 'spiders' of government, industry, and corporations. I see their powers, but I now also see their weaknesses. Through research and investigation I now see a way to resist and challenge those weaknesses and begin the work necessary to collapse those webs. Will I live to see the realisation of that work? Probably not. But maybe one day in the not too distant future someone with a keen interest in the history and the politics of animal liberation will pull my dusty tome from a shelf, where for many a year it will have sheltered generations of arachnids, and they will read words of a revolution gone by and will use them to fire their fight for a better future.

If you are reading this, you now have the foundational knowledge to be an animal advocate, or to be a more effective strategist for other animals. I have not provided all the answers; no one person can. But I feel I have posed enough questions for the animal advocate to pursue in ways that are now clearer to them. If you would like a more tangible take-away that isn't a long list of questions, I would like to leave you with a five stage approach that we can all undertake with ease:

1. Recognise other animals as leaders at the helm of their own movement for liberation

2. Kill the activist identity and move towards activism as praxis

3. Create communities, including among those who seem the unlikeliest of allies

4. Embrace mutual aid as an applicable framework for liberation over consumerism

5. Go vegan if you are not already, and if you are vegan get political!

As daunting as this task may appear, we must remember that progress is always possible. And those who say "it cannot be done" will invariably be interrupted by those of us who are already sprinting headlong into the future.

References

Allen, M., & von Essen, E. (2018). Animal resistors: On the right of resistance and human duties of non-return and abolition. *Journal for Critical Animal Studies, 15*(6), 4-30.

Ankel, S. (2020). *A pod of killer whales is accused of 'orchestrated' attacks on boats, terrifying the sailors and baffling scientists.* https://www.businessinsider.com.au/orcas-ramming-boats-in-portugal-spain-unusual-display-of-behavior-2020-9

Farm Transparency Project (2020). *Cow escapes Kankool Pet Meat slaughterhouse.* https://www.facebook.com/FarmTransparencyProject/videos/1035059263573163

Higgins, P. (2010). *Eradicating ecocide: Laws and governance to prevent the destruction of our planet.* Shepheard-Walwyn Publishers.

Intergovernmental Science-Policy Platform on Biodiversity and Ecosystem Services (2019). *UN report: Nature's dangerous decline 'unprecedented': Species extinction rates 'accelerating'.* https://www.un.org/sustainabledevelopment/blog/2019/05/nature-decline-unprecedented-report/

Moore, J. (2016). The rise of cheap nature. In J. Moore (Ed.), *Anthropocene or Capitalocene? Nature, history, and the crisis of capitalism* (pp. 78-116). PM Press.

Plutarch (c.100ce/1998). *Greek lives.* (Trans. Robert Waterfield). Oxford University Press.

Smillie, S. (2020). *Scientists baffled by orcas ramming sailing boats near Spain and Portugal.* https://www.theguardian.com/environment/2020/sep/13/killer-whales-launch-orchestrated-attacks-on-sailing-boats

subversive energy (2012). *Beyond animal liberation.* https://theanarchistlibrary.org/library/subversive-energy-beyond-animal-liberation

Twine,
R. (2012). Revealing the 'animal-industrial complex': A concept and method for critical animal studies. *Journal for Critical Animal Studies, 10*(1), 12-39.

Appendix

Appendix 1: Hansard 31/10/2019
Dog Control Amendment Bill 2019 (No. 43): Second Reading

a. Minister for Primary Industries Guy Barnett

I will speak more of the particular provisions with respect to the bill but I would like to commence by drawing the House's attention to the contribution of the Labor shadow minister for local government and planning during debate on this bill yesterday. During her contribution, Ms. Dow quoted extensively from Animal Liberation Tasmania, a group of extreme animal rights activists with a track record of deliberately disrupting the daily lives of everyday Tasmanians and an agenda which destroys jobs across regional and rural communities. Animal Liberation Tasmania activists have attached themselves to the Tasman Bridge, causing traffic chaos. They have occupied public buildings and disrupted workplaces, including at the Tasmanian Quality Meats abattoir in Cressy. Animal Liberation Tasmania's sister organisation on the mainland has closed down CBD streets and occupied abattoirs and farms across Victoria, New South Wales and Queensland, resulting in scores of arrests and criminal charges.

It is all on the public record. It is on the *Hansard*. Ms. Dow has used her arguments in support of our bill quoting the Animal Liberation Tasmania submission. She has quoted [...]

[interjection]

I am making an observation with respect to Animal Liberation Tasmania and their sister organisations on the mainland. I recognise and acknowledge The Greens. They have been consistent in their support for Animal Liberation Tasmania and their sister organisation to protest, to be disruptive, to cause civil disobedience, and to be arrested and subjected to criminal charges. I acknowledge that from The Greens. You have been consistent.

Frankly it beggars belief that a Labor Member for Braddon, where agriculture is so foundational to that community, the support for rural and regional jobs in Braddon on the North West coast of Tasmania, would seek to […]

[interjection]

I can see how sensitive the Member for Braddon is about this matter.

It beggars belief that they come here using arguments from Animal Liberation Tasmania to support the views of the Labor Party. This is the Labor Party that stands shoulder to shoulder, like they did in government, Labor and Greens in government for four years. This place went into recession. We lost 10 000 jobs. Agriculture and rural and regional communities were devastated under Labor and the Greens.

The evidence is on the public record; it is on the *Hansard* for all to see. The Member for Braddon, Ms. Dow, was in here yesterday, quoting from the Animal Liberation Tasmania submission.

She was using that submission to support her position on behalf of the Labor Party. As Minister for Primary Industries and Water, it is cause for grave concern that a Member for Braddon, where agriculture is so important, has caused much disruption. She knows full well that Animal Liberation Tasmania has caused much damage to the reputation for agriculture. This is with their sister organisations on the mainland.

I am expressing that concern on the public record. You came in here on the public record. I am putting on the public record my concerns. What it says here is that Labor and The Greens are so close in their relationship that they are using the same arguments. I respect The Greens. They have a position. As the leader of The Greens has indicated, they fully support Animal Liberation Tasmania and their sister organisations on the mainland. Here we have a Labor Member for Braddon, where agriculture is so important – frankly it beggars belief that a member would do such a thing. I call on the Member for Braddon to condemn Animal Liberation Tasmania and their activities. Will you do that? Absolute silence. She said nothing. It is on the public record that the Member for Braddon has been silent when asked whether she will condemn the activities of Animal Liberation Tasmania […]

[interjection]

I was asking a rhetorical question and I heard nothing. A vacuous nothing from the other side. Absolutely nothing. I ask her to express support for rural and regional agricultural Tasmania.

We have done so much on this side of the House. I am not going to have it jeopardised by people on the other side in the Labor Party when it comes to Animal Liberation Tasmania. I will not stand for it. You stand up. Let the Labor Party express their views. The shadow minister came in here, quoting from Animal Liberation Tasmania, using their submission, using their arguments. Let us hear about it. You can put your views forwards on the adjournment, or publicly outside this place. I ask you to condemn the position. I ask you to condemn the activities Animal Liberation Tasmania that have caused so much damage to the reputation of agriculture in Tasmania and across the country. That is my position. I put it on record. Let us see what Labor do about it.

Appendix 2: Hansard 27/11/2019
Workplaces (Protection from Protestors) Amendment Bill 2019

a. Minister for Primary Industries, Guy Barnett

Across the country we have seen people attempting to physically shut down shops by blockading entrances, mass trespasses on farms, and roads and railways being blocked. These types of behaviour are unacceptable and our laws must clearly support people who are going about their lawful business.

The Bill creates offences for trespassers who intentionally

impede business activity on business premises or on, or in, a business vehicle. While there are already offences for trespass in Tasmanian law, trespass aggravated by the intentional impediment of business activity has the potential to cause significant economic loss for workers and businesses. For that reason, the Bill makes these offences subject to a maximum penalty of 18 months' imprisonment for a first offence and four years' imprisonment for a further offence. This will provide the country's highest maximum penalty for the offence of trespass while intentionally impeding business activity on business premises.

b. Former Premier, Will Hodgman

It is a bill that is supported by, amongst others, the TFGA, the TCCI, FIAT, the Tasmanian Minerals, Manufacturing and Energy Council, the Tasmanian Seafood Industry Council, and the Tasmanian Small Business Council. That is who we will be standing alongside, and standing up for today with respect to the legislation.

c. Cassy O'Connor, The Greens

This legislation, a bill of rights for business, on its merits, is an insult to our democracy. It is an insult to free-thinking people everywhere. It is an insult to the generations of Tasmanians who have stood up for what is good and true and for their rights and workers' rights.

Section II of the principal act has been removed so there is, now, not even a requirement for police to ask people to move before they arrest them and potentially send them to jail for 18 months for the first offence.

The minister says in his second reading speech that more than 400 submissions were received in response to the bill, but the Department of Justice website displays each of the submissions. Can you confirm that only two support-ive submissions were received; one from the Tasmanian Minerals and Energy Council and the second from an indi-vidual Tasmanian resident, Mr. Trustrum?

> d. Michelle O'Byrne, Labor

The third part is subclause (c), which makes it very clear that the only lawful action is going to be granted by a permit. Well, that clears that up, doesn't it? The only protests that will be permitted in our state are the ones permitted by the Government. Any action without a permit is illegal, and any action that falls outside of that permit while the action is being undertaken is also illegal.

If somebody threatens to undertake an act, and then does not undertake the act, they are convicted as if they had under-taken the act.

> e. Joan Rylah, former Liberal Minister (founder of
> pro-development group Unlock Tasmania and
> a beef farmer)

The militant agenda is an agenda of the privileged, the modern elite, who, in no way different to that of feudal times, demean and suck the lifeblood out of everyday people, whom they look down their noses at and trample underfoot.

f. Brian Tucker, Liberal Minister (Government Whip and Parliamentary Secretary to the Premier)

The upsurge in targeted actions follows the unleashing of a new activist philosophy that might be modelled on the shock-and-awe tactics employed in the Gulf War.

Appendix 3: Hansard 21/10/2019
Agriculture Long-Term Plan

a. Minister for Primary Industries, Guy Barnett

We are working shoulder-to-shoulder with the Tasmanian Farmers and Graziers Association and the Tasmanian Agricultural Productivity Group.

Appendix 4: Interview with Ms. Leni Descalle (name changed for security) 11/11/2020
Spectacled and Little Red Flying-Fox Dispersals, Cairns & Mareeba QLD

1. *How long have you been an observer at the 2020 dispersal?*

I have been documenting the Cairns City Library dispersal since the 4th of July 2020. And more recently spent three days in Mareeba.

2. *What have you seen occur at both the Cairns library site and the more recent dispersal actions at Mareeba?*

The use of LRAD devices emitting gun fire, canon sounds, high pitched tones, animal sounds for extended periods of time. In combination with direct high powered torch light including strobe function. Daylight flood lighting directed in areas flying foxes would otherwise settle and roost. Bashing together of metal rods, pool noodles, wooden planks, and more recently a clicker device.

I have seen workers show little regard for the highly sensitive sight and hearing of the spectacled flying-foxes. Use of equipment in close proximity to animals. Use of dispersal methods repeatedly and for extended periods of time. I have witnessed distressed and exhausted animals trying to re-land, indicating fatigue or disorientation. I have witnessed a massive change in behaviour [of the flying-foxes]. In the early days animals would try to stay and withstand even the most intense and horrific use of sound and light harassment. Now almost five months later, hundreds of flying-foxes can lift [leave the roost] with the smallest of sounds, potentially indicating long-term trauma and increased sensitivity and fear. These animals were very accustomed to loud noise in an urban environment.

In Mareeba the use of loud birdfrite shots, and a sort of noise firework/flare type sound and light deterrent to "herd" thousands of little red flying foxes in a desired direction. Animals appear to lose sense of direction, often splitting up as a colony, circling in several directions. Landing and being dispersed again. This dispersal was done right after bushfires impacted the area.

3. *Have there been injuries or deaths of adults and pups?*

At 135 days, 51 orphaned pups, 6 dead adults. Though council reports deaths and injuries cannot be linked to the dispersal. These numbers are significantly lower than previous years at this camp, but the deaths in the region as a whole are higher. The council will not acknowledge the data as being related.

We have also documented a flying-fox mother giving birth during the dispersal at the library, only to be scared away a few hours later. We don't know what happened to the pup.

4. *What has the response been from:*

a. local government representatives

Local government relies on statistics from a time when they approved several building works in close proximity to the colony, as well as ignoring their own removal of 42 significant roost trees over the years, to claim that this is an unsafe and at risk camp. There have been high fatalities at this camp, but council has never committed to improving conditions here, only taken actions to place it at higher risk. Their response has been one of creating and maintaining a narrative and hiding/lying to the public when it comes to voice evidence that contradicts this.

b. wildlife carers called in to assist

The caring community largely initially supported the dispersal as they had just been through a terrible season of casualties at this camp. They are of the opinion that construction works approved in the area (2 new massive hotels) and more removal of surrounding trees meant this camp was no longer suitable and it was worth trying to get them somewhere safer. Their support changed as soon as the birthing season arrived and the council continued to push ahead. This was early September. There is still however some conflict, as a team of carers is being paid to assist at the dispersal site.

c. the media

Community/media interest has been minimal as the council has done a very good job at portraying this as a success, despite the obvious harm caused and the worrying trends emerging in deaths across the region, and the moving of camps and inability for flying-foxes to form a stable crèche colony to raise their pups. This was in previous years always at the library site.

d. the broader community

Community is divided. Those educated on the importance of this species and who have a general respect for nature appreciate them [flying-foxes] whole heartedly. Those who are uneducated on the part they [flying-foxes] play in the ecosystem choose to focus on the simple narrative that they shit and piss and it stinks, and that they carry diseases and that's where corona virus came from etc.

e. What sort of language have you heard or seen used regarding the flying-foxes themselves?

Rats with wings, filthy, pests, diseased, ugly, smelly, flying cane toads.